Shrouded in Darkness

Phyllis Popovich

authorHOUSE®

AuthorHouse™
1663 Liberty Drive, Suite 200
Bloomington, IN 47403
www.authorhouse.com
Phone: 1-800-839-8640

First published by AuthorHouse 8/21/2008

ISBN: 978-1-4343-9230-5 (sc)

Library of Congress Control Number: 2008905449

Printed in the United States of America
Bloomington, Indiana

This book is printed on acid-free paper.

Bible versions used:

King James Version

Isaiah 60:2

For, behold, the darkness shall cover the earth, and gross darkness the people: but, the Lord shall arise upon thee, and his glory shall be seen upon thee.

TABLE OF CONTENTS

DEDICATION

Deepest appreciation and thanks to all who encouraged me to write this book and prayed for me as I did. I could not have done it without them. It is dedicated, as well, to all the brave heroes and heroines of the cross, who have willingly given themselves to serve the Lord, body, soul and spirit; and, to the martyrs, both Christian and Jew, throughout the centuries.

Most of all this work is dedicated to Jesus Christ, my Lord and Savior, the Lamb of God, who called me out of darkness into His marvelous light, and who shall one day soon reign over all the earth as King of kings and Lord of lords, bringing an end to all mankind's evil, and Satan's demonic devices once and for all.

PREFACE

On New Year's Eve 1990, I heard the sound of a shofar. The shofar, or ram's horn, was used to call Israel to assemble for battle. I first heard it during a visitation from the Lord in 1972. It was a call to sound an alarm. With this book, I am sounding that alarm.

> *Blow ye the trumpet in Zion, and sound an alarm in my holy mountain: let all the inhabitants of the land tremble: for the day of the LORD cometh, for it is nigh at hand; a day of darkness and of gloominess, a day of clouds and of thick darkness and of gloominess, a day of clouds and of thick darkness, as the morning spread upon the mountains: a great people and a strong; there hath not been ever the like, neither shall be any more after it, even to the years of many generations.*
>
> (Joel 2:1-2)

Always one to want truth, I found the truth in 1954 at a small, white church in Colorado. The pastor preached Jesus, the head of the body. Knowing I was not a part of that body, I wept bitterly over my sins at the altar that October morning and received Jesus as my Savior.

I wandered in the wilderness for several years until I received the gift of the Holy Spirit in 1961. Several more years were spent in that vast wilderness of trial and testing; but, never without an extreme hunger for more of God.

In 1972, many were stating the rapture theory

was wrong, and the church would go through the Great Tribulation. Determined to know the truth, I prayed and fasted seeking the answer to this age-old question. It was then the Lord confirmed His calling. Over a period of several weeks, two Bible verses were repeatedly impressed on my spirit. I realized these verses were specific to the call of God on my life.

> *O daughter of my people, gird thee with sackcloth, and wallow thyself in ashes: make thee mourning, as for an only son, most bitter lamentation: for the spoiler shall suddenly come upon us. I have set thee for a tower and a fortress among my people, that thou mayest know and try their way.*
>
> (Jeremiah 6:26-27)

I have come to recognize God called me to be a watchman for the body of Christ, and the assignment was to intercede for the church…exposing, whenever necessary, deception. At the end of that '72 fast, I also had the following nighttime visitation:

> There was a long blast of a horn. I thought it was a factory whistle, or something of that nature, as I had never before heard that strange sound. (I later learned it was the Israelite's shofar horn.) The horn's blast was followed by a series of five numbers, "9, 12, 15, 18, 21," with the words, "Go over them again, again and again. Go over them again, again and again." I awoke, startled, but quickly went back to sleep. Again, I heard the horn's blast and the numbers, "9, 12, 15, 18, 21,"

followed by the words, "Go over them again, again and again."

Nine, I discovered. was the number of finality, and Satan's influence was about to be unleashed in greater measure upon the church and political arena.

On September 11, 1990,[1] George H. W. Bush announced a decision to "check the aggression" of Iraq into Saudi Arabia. Operation Desert Storm was underway. Nine, the number of finality, was about to begin; but, not before other events of historical proportions would erupt on the world scene.

Nine...9, Hebrew, *tet*, surround or snake

Dr. Bullinger states in his book *Number in Scripture*:

> The number nine is…held in great reverence by all who study the occult sciences; and in mathematical science, it possesses properties and powers which are found in no other number. It is the last of the digits, and thus marks the *end*; and is significant of the conclusion of a matter.

> It is akin to the number *six*, six being the sum of its factors ($3 \times 3 = 9$ and $3 + 3 = 6$), and is thus significant of the *end of man*, and the summation of man's works. Nine is therefore, THE NUMBER OF FINALITY OR JUDGMENT.[2]

Twelve...12, Hebrew, *lamed*, teacher or purpose

Bullinger states:

Twelve is a perfect number, signifying

perfection of government, or *government perfection.* It is found as a multiple in all that has to do with *rule....* Twelve is the product of 3, (the perfectly Divine and heavenly number) and 4 (the earthly, the number of what is material and organic).

While seven is composed of 3 *added* to 4, twelve is 3 *multiplied* by 4, and hence denotes that which can scarcely be explained in words, but which the spiritual perception can at once appreciate....[3]

Jews read from right to left; in this way, 2 plus 1 equals 3, another perfect number, and the number of the triune God...God the Father, Son and Holy Ghost. Twelve is observed throughout Scripture as in the 12 apostles, the 12 sons of Jacob, and quite prominent within the New Jerusalem which descends from heaven as revealed in Revelation 21:12-21.

Twelve, I believe, represents the rebuilding of the temple in the old city of Jerusalem. *"...which spiritually is called Sodom and Egypt...."* (Revelation 11:8) Presently, the Levitical priesthood is training to perform animal sacrifices once again in accordance with Old Testament laws. These sacrifices are intended to be held in this newly constructed temple.

The reference could apply to the believer, as well, those in whose temple (body) the Holy Spirit resides. This temple must be found of Jesus *"...without spot or wrinkle...."* (Ephesians 5:27) and willingly conform to His perfect governmental will and standards when He comes for His bride, who will make up the New Jerusalem.

Fifteen…15, Hebrew, *samech*, divine protection or support

Bullinger continues:

Fifteen, being a multiple of *five*, partakes of the significance of that number, also of the number *three* with which it is combined, 3 x 5.

Five is… the number of *grace*, and *three* is the number of *divine perfection*. *Fifteen*, therefore, specially refers to acts wrought by the energy of divine grace.…

The number *fifteen* is thus made up, by addition, 10 + 5; but as the Jews would not, by the constant use of these two letters, profane the sacred name, two other letters were arbitrarily used for this number.…[4]

The factor of three times five (15) reveals God's marvelous acts coupled with His grace. While *tet*, the Hebrew number 9, and *vau*, Hebrew for number 6, together add up to 15. Bullinger does not see any significance in this use of 9 + 6 equaling 15. However, nine, the number of the snake, or surrounded by the snake, and six, the number of man without God, shows the restrainer no longer holding back lawlessness; hence, full release of the Antichrist spirit.

These numbers added side by side, 1 + 5 = 6, bring us to the middle number of the five numbers in the visitation. I believe this indicates the middle of the Great Tribulation and the rise of Antichrist, whose purpose is to rule the world by manipulation, control and force, declaring himself, God

For those remaining on earth during this period of temptation, be they a Jew or Gentile believer, God will continue to provide His ultimate protection and provision as they keep centered on Him and His promises. Nevertheless, it will be a time of extreme persecution and/or martyrdom for any one who opposes the Antichrist and his subordinates. During this time of trial and tribulation, through the sacrificial lives and testimonies of the saints, many lost souls will come to saving grace in Jesus Christ.

Eighteen…18, Hebrew, *tzaddi*, for home

Bullinger is silent on the number 18, a combination of 10 and 8. Ten is the number of ordinal perfection, i.e., the Ten Commandments, and eight, the number of superabundance. It is a time of divine rule and new beginnings. Seven comprises the notes of a scale, colors in the rainbow, days of a week, etc., while eight starts the pattern all over again.

Eighteen most likely represents the time of the millennial kingdom…a time of God's loving dominion over mankind with ordinal perfection…a theocratic society ruled by none other than Jesus Christ as King of kings and Lord of lords. During this period those who have suffered with Christ will rule and reign with Him.

Adding 1 + 8, again is the number 9, or finality, the windup of all things, or at home with the Lord, since *tzaddi* means home.

Twenty-one…21, Hebrew, *shin*, the person and character of God; city of God and peace

Again, Bullinger is silent on 21. God's mathematical

equations are profound! There is nothing lacking in His order. Twenty-one is 3 x 7, regarded as two perfect numbers. Three equals divine perfection, and seven, spiritual perfection. Thus, we come to God's perfect finale of that which encompasses the entire Bible and which concludes the revelation of Jesus Christ and establishment of a new heaven and a new earth. Refer to Revelation 21 and 22 regarding the subject of a new heaven and a new earth; and, the New Jerusalem coming down from heaven as a bride prepared for her husband. .

Unquenched Zeal

My zeal for the Lord has never stopped. My childhood was filled with a love for mystery and intrigue as I was raised by a father who loved the same. He inspired me to seek answers in response to a questioning mind. Because of this, during the election in which Nixon was running against Wallace, as a "dyed in the wool" Republican, I decided for the first time in my thirty-five years, to find out what the other side had to say. What a surprise it was when I learned elections, even here in the United States, were "rigged."

At the Democratic Headquarters, I was given a book called, *None Dare Call It Treason*, by John A. Stormer. An avid reader, I took it home and read it straight through, taking only a short time out to catch my breath. The book dealt with a "shadow government", which, under cover of closeted doors, directed all aspects of governmental affairs, and those who could be bought and readily condescend to work with it. These subversives picked and chose individuals they considered the best candidates to carry out their futuristic aims.

Incredulous, my eyes were opened, I would never see things the same again. I would later learn that in reality we had no two-party system…that was a sham foisted on an unwary populace. For both parties were basically working toward the establishment of a One World government, even at that early date. The 1972 visitation was an awakening for me to sound an alarm…the alarm of an emerging apostasy…both spiritual and political.

Like many, I had never heard of the word apostasy, until Jim Spellman, a Sunday school teacher told our '60s class that apostasy would be one of the last, great signs of the coming of the Lord. The word grabbed my attention and from that day forward I have watched the downward spiral and decadence both within the church and the government. While this was occurring, there appeared to be true believers and morally upright citizens, who were attempting to make known their concern, but these were over ridden by media propaganda and hype.

In confirmation of my findings, over a span of several years, I had three significant dreams, included here. The first of these deal with Israel and Iraq, and preparations for a council of 10.

Dream Number One: Shortly before or after midnight, December 31, 1990

I was in what appeared to be a kitchen. Everything was pushed up against the west wall. This included awards and trophies in a case high up on the wall. There was a window covered over by the things pushed up against that wall. I especially noted a long, heavy, wooden table, with no chairs and nothing on it. It, too, was pushed up against the wall.

As the scene changed, the table moved from the west to the north, there were still no chairs. Next, this rectangular table moved further east. The short widths of the table were on the east and west, and the longer sides to the north and south. It was shaped like a rectangle, with the west end rounded and the east end squared. The table was almost invisible in extremely tall grass. There were five chairs on either side, all empty.

The picture changed again, and I was standing beneath a large, tall tree, holding three packs of playing cards of 52 each. As I looked at them, they fell on the ground spread out in the shape of a fish. I heard the words, "Pick up." I began wrapping bits of what appeared to be food in aluminum foil and placing these morsels above my head as I heard the words, "Wrap up."

Interpretation: Israel is backed up against the wall; everything they treasure pushed out of place, and they can see no way out; many yet have to receive the light of the knowledge of Jesus, the Light of the World, as their Messiah.

The table moving to the north indicated the nations to their north were "tabling" things in preparation to act against the nation of Israel. The northern army was laying plans to march against Israel with their Arab allies, as in Ezekiel 38 and 39---the battle of Gog and Magog.

Then, the table was moved toward the east. The tall grass surrounding it was reminiscent of Nebuchadnezzar's reign, when he was punished by the Lord. This predicted our present involvement with Iraq; and, the ten chairs, representative of the ten kings, who may come out of the revised Roman Empire (the European Common Market).

And the ten horns which thou sawest are ten kings, which have received no kingdom as yet; but receive power as kings one hour with the beast. These have one mind, and shall give their power and strength unto the beast.

(Revelation 17:12-13)

The rounded west end left no place for a chair; evidently, the West, normally considered the United States, will not take part in this end-time scenario, as the "elitists" plan to demoralize and wipe out our culture. The tables represent events which will eventually culminate in the Middle East, with a pseudo-peace placing Israel in great jeopardy.

The cards represent a period of time (in the dream I knew the timing, but not when I awoke), or the days of prophecy quickly playing out and picking up on a daily basis. The last part of the dream was a reminder to lay up our treasures in heaven.

Dream Number Two: December 3, 1992

The scene was that of a huge Christian gathering. Those attending were rejoicing, praising the Lord, and enjoying the time of fellowship with other believers. Above, storm clouds began to gather. The skies became black and foreboding. As the clouds became dense and extremely thick and dark, the crowd began to disperse, each going their separate ways.

At this point I was alone, attempting to press my way through the blackness with my hands palm to palm in the form we recognize as praying hands. I was using them to chop my way through the heavy, thick darkness. The atmosphere appeared so heavy it was like plowing through heavy cotton batting or construction insulation. There was no way to see the way home, it was entirely too dark and threatening.

My "chopping" positioned me before a crumbling brick wall at eye level. I could not see what was on the floor above the wall. At this height, the bricks were placed on end, making a border that appeared something like this: /\/\/\/\/\/\/\/\/\/\/\/\/\, spread further apart.

Suddenly, I found myself above the wall on a crumbling, uneven, cement floor. On that floor was wobbly, heavy, branch-type furniture, like those pieces seen in the southern states. This furniture was weak; the legs on each piece whitewashed. To my right, looking east was a canopy over an empty dirt lot. Under this canopy a man was hoeing in the dirt. It was implied in the dream that he wanted me to remain there. I replied, "No, I'm going home."

Interpretation: Many mega churches and gigantic seminars were meeting oblivious to the gathering storm. When it finally struck, the only way to safety was through fervent, intercessory prayer, and that prayer was an individual responsibility.

The wall, floor and furniture are types of the burgeoning government that is shaky at best and will not last. Known as the New World Order, it will ultimately be destroyed, along with the New Age church movement. (See Revelation 17 and 18) The man to the east represents the appearance of the Antichrist, encouraging believers to side with him…take his mark. His appearance revealed the time for the coming of Jesus Christ and our home going.

Dream Number Three: June 1994

I was outside a large, white, frame house, which looked to be three stories high. On one side were two stately trees. They appeared to be either cedar or oak. As I watched, the first one toppled, jarring the roof of the white house and inflicting damage to the roof. The house was not destroyed and could still be occupied.

I turned to look behind me. Gardeners were working on the landscape of a newer cement structure. I went inside. More men were laying red carpeting on the floors and the entryway. I went inside to the large picture window and looked out.

The second tree, which had a large section cut out about three-quarters of the way through the tree and near the bottom, fell over with a large crash. It shook the white house severely; and, it could no longer be occupied in that condition.

As I continued to gaze out the window, I noticed another tall tree. It appeared to be a eucalyptus tree with various colored bark. There were several green shoots on this tree, its tree roots were very shallow; and, it grew far away from the rest of the scene.

In the new structure, tables were being set up with red tablecloths, and several people preparing to serve.

Interpretation: The two stately trees appear to represent the Republican and Democratic parties…both weak structurally. The first tree's fall (the Republican Party) was when George H. W. Bush, during his inauguration address used the term, "a thousand points of light," indicating a New World Order was about to begin. This phrase is a term well understood by occultists, Illuminati initiates, and those who want a Fourth Reich.

G.H.W. Bush was the first president in the White House to mention the establishment of a New World Order. During his term in office, the roof of the White House was damaged…our Republic in deep trouble.

When the second tree crashed to the ground, it apparently was when Tom Foley, former Speaker of the House during Clinton's administration, was accused of felony theft and other crimes. (This signified the cut in the trunk of the tree, and represented the Democratic Party's toppling.) This second tree fell across the highway and required much debris to be cleared away.

During the Clinton administration, a cement abutment was put on the road in front of the White House for protection. Clinton's term as president brought chaos. It required removal of much trash, but prepared the way for a more destructive political system, of which he is very much a part. Clinton's many Executive Orders have placed us squarely in the United Nations' camp, and may have changed our government forever.

The third tree depicts all the other minor parties and/or candidates attempting to make an impact on the political front; i.e., the green shoots on the eucalyptus tree, shallow of root with little or no effect on the future of the United States.

The newer structure has quickly formed under George W. Bush. His presidency has led us squarely into the New World Order, which will be hard and unfeeling, rigid and cold. This structure gives a façade of being beautiful, when, in fact, it is a cold, hard and unbending structure, whose foundation is covered by red carpeting to hide its foundational flaws. (The color red is common in despotic kingdoms…Socialist, Communistic or Fascist.) This rigid, cold structure is nearing completion. Glamorized to appear good to the eye, it depicts a new government, much like Nazi Germany.

Quest for Truth

Propaganda is served daily through the news media, causing the populace to be misled concerning the subtle loss of freedom. The elderly longingly recall the days they could walk down a city street day or night without the danger of being mugged. While crime and violence has increased in dramatic proportions; most are in denial, believing things the same as they once were, or as mistakenly taught in their churches, are going to get better. As Mathew Henry said: "There's none so blind as those who will not see."

Streets are filled with hordes of people, their faces no longer full of smiles or with a cordial greetings on their lips; their countenance gives evidence of worry, confusion, bitterness or anger. Racial tensions have increased, leading the different cultures to turn against each other. As a result, gang wars prevail throughout metropolitian areas. Wars and rumors of war are fought in countries worldwide. Famine, fires, earthquakes and other major disasters have become commonplace, as the prophecies of Matthew 24, Mark 13, and Luke 21 are fulfilled daily.

The majority of people find it hard to believe that there is a conspiracy afoot. However, this book is about a conspiracy that began as early as the Garden of Eden. It is an attempt to reveal the inner workings of a Luciferian plan for a One World Government under a One World Church, all supposedly to usher in a New Age…a Utopia made by man…one in which they hope to omit the Lord Himself. This, Lucifer has worked diligently to perform using ungodly men, bent on hell, willing to serve in satanic evil secret societies.

This book endeavors to show the reader the workings of a minute few of these evil organizations, including the Illuminati, Freemasonry and the Orientis Templi Ordo.

This was not a book I wanted to write. In fact, if the Lord hadn't been so insistent through the urgings of His still, small voice, His Word, and through several of His anointed messengers, I would have easily laid it aside on numerous occasions, as the enemy which I have attempted to expose, did everything in his power to oppose the work. But, thanks be to God, for what He begins, He also completes, even through the weakest vessel. .

My greatest desire by writing this book is that the reader will see the days in which we now live as being under the control, not of the enemy, but of God Himself. It is intended to enlighten the reader as to the satanic conspiracy that has brought about worldwide apostasy; and, is meant to expose the darkness, causing many to turn from the wicked devices of Satan to a loving, all-wise God. God foreknew the evil plans and all their evil works, and through His Word has given ample warning to those who will listen.

In His time, He will quickly bring to an end all their wicked devices, as has been prophesied by the prophets of both New and Old Testaments. Yes, all that is happening is not ushering in man's Utopia, but the revelation of Jesus Christ, His rule and reign over His Kingdom.

May God open your spiritual eyes and understanding and reveal to you the necessity of accepting the plan of God and arming yourself with His Word to rise above all obstacles and be victorious in Him.

This book is intended to enlighten the reader as to the satanic conspiracy that has brought about this apostasy; and, meant to expose the darkness, to turn many souls from the wicked devices of Satan to a loving, all-wise God.

Most of all, this work is dedicated to Jesus Christ, my Lord and Savior, the Lamb of God, who called me out of darkness into His marvelous light; and who shall one day soon reign over all the earth as King of kings and Lord of lords, bringing an end to all of mankind's evil, and Satan's demonic devices once and for all.

"CRY," He said,
"What shall I cry?" I asked.
"For wisdom, understanding, and knowledge," He
replied.
"For lack of knowledge, My people perish."

"WRITE," He said.
"What shall I write?" I asked.
"Write all I give you, and keep back nothing," He
replied.

"WATCH," He said.
"How shall I watch?" I asked.
"By seeking My face to enquire of the night.

"PRAY," He said.
"How shall I pray?" I asked.
"Pray always that ye may be accounted worthy to
escape the things to come to pass on the face of
the earth and to stand before the Son of Man."

"STAND," He said.
"How shall I stand?" I asked.
"Upon My Word in truth and in righteousness."

"TRUST," He said.
"How do I trust?" I asked.
"By leaning on Me and My Word amid
perplexities."

THE ARM OF FLESH SHALL FAIL YOU,
YE DARE NOT TRUST YOUR OWN.

Phyllis Popovich...1993

CHAPTER ONE

ANCIENT WISDOM

There is a way which seemeth right unto a man, but the ends thereof are the ways of death.

(Proverbs 14:120

What a legacy those two had! They would endow the earth with saints and sinners alike. Their seed would bring dividends, both good and evil. Soon after their sin, Eve gave birth to her first son, Cain. She thought he was a blessing from God, and remarked, *"I have gotten a man from the LORD."* (Genesis 4:1). Eve was still deceived. Cain didn't have the heart of his father, Adam, or of God, but, the heart of a murderer.

Some Bible scholars believe fallen angels had intercourse with the daughters of men in early history. (See Genesis 6:2-4) So, it is quite possible that Satan was the father of Cain. We may never know for certain, but an evil seed has passed down from generation to generation until the present day. Perhaps, it was Cain's ancestry that Jesus referred to when He rebuked the Pharisees.

Ye are of your father the devil, and the lusts of your father ye will do. He was a murderer from the beginning, and abode not in the truth, because there is no truth in him. When he speaketh a lie, he speaketh of his own: for he is a liar, and the father of it.

(John 8:44)

Centuries later, a prince would claim he received his crown from his father; when, in fact, it was inherited from the queen mother; and, it was she who placed the crown upon his head. One should ask: Who was he referring to as his father? His investiture came under the national symbol of Wales---a fiery red dragon. Under that banner, the young prince was given *"...power, and his seat, and great authority."* (Revelation 13:2)

Many have come to suspect that this is indeed the man who will one day take his place in the temple proclaiming himself as God...the Antichrist.[5] Their suspicions are not unfounded, for the prince and his entire family are participants in occult ceremonies which have evolved from the Ancient Mysteries directed by Satan, the Light Bearer, and overlord of the cult of the All-Seeing Eye, Satan is still the source of the knowledge of good and evil. His followers are known to practice both.

When Adam and Eve were deceived, their third-eye opened. Some call it clairvoyance; or, as the serpent called it, the knowledge of good and evil. Even, with all their newly discovered knowledge, they immediately realized their betrayal of God. The seed of their deception was "cover-up," a hallmark of sinners in every walk of life.

The evil seed implanted within Cain took root. When Cain and Abel made their sacrifices to God, the difference in them became strongly apparent. Abel sacrificed an unblemished, irreplaceable lamb from his flock; Cain, in rebellion, chose a sacrifice from the *cursed ground.*

Abel's murder was the first incident where the power of blood was revealed. Abel's blood cried from the ground and alerted the Lord to Cain's sin. It was Abel who wore the first martyr's crown.

And Cain talked with Abel his brother: and it came to pass, when they were in the field, that Cain rose up against Abel his brother, and slew him. And the LORD said unto Cain, Where is Abel thy brother? And he said, I know not: Am I my brother's keeper? And he said, What hast thou done? The voice of thy brother's blood crieth unto me from the ground.

(Genesis 4:8-10)

God placed a mark upon Cain and commanded him to depart. Cain left, going east, where he built a city called Nod, which means, "wandering." He and his family would be nomads the remainder of their lives. Josephus relates that Cain didn't learn from his banishment.

However he did not accept of his punishment in order to amendment, but to increase his wickedness; for he only aimed to procure everything that was for his own bodily pleasure, though it obliged him to be injurious to his neighbours.... And, whereas they lived innocently and generously while they knew nothing of such arts, he changed the world into cunning craftiness.[6]

Cain was guilty of hedonism---the love of pleasure---anything that pleased his senses. He lived for himself, independent of God, and felt he was perfectly capable of handling his own life---humanistic. He was devious and crafty, having all he attributes of rebellious humanity.

Cain's son, Tubal, according to Josephus, "...

exceeded all men in strength, and was very expert and famous in *martial performances*."[7] Martial arts were in existence at the time of Nimrod. These "arts" require deep concentration and can open the mind to delusion; and, in some cases, demon possession. Martial arts work through the power of the soul, which wars against the spirit. The soul not controlled by God is an open door to demonic activity. Martial arts are one subtle form of indoctrination into the New Age belief system.

Josephus further states, "…the posterity of Cain became exceedingly wicked, every one successively dying more wicked than the former."[8] There is really nothing new under the sun. For the pride, jealousy and murder Cain had chosen, continued its course; and, like a boil coming to a head, is now ready to be lanced.

Perverse Wisdom

Cain and his heirs developed a strange, ancient religion…a philosophy closely related to the plan of God, but entirely perverse. It became known as "the craft," Luciferian Gnosticism,[9] higher knowledge, or higher consciousness, also referred to as Ancient Wisdom; and, which was retrieved by the Jewish cabala.[10].

> The commonly used term for the mystical, magical, and theosophic teachings of Judaism from the twelfth century onward, the cabala (also cabbala, **kabbala**, or kabbalah) was considered the esoteric and **unwritten** portion of the revelation granted to Adam and again to Moses, while the Bible represented the **exoteric** revelation. (Although the term is often spelled with a "k" when referring

4

to the Jewish tradition and with a "c" in the Christian version, it is spelled here with a "c" for simplicity's sake.) The word means "that which is received" or "tradition," implying that the cabala was a body of knowledge that passed orally from generation to generation.[11]

It could be referred to as *revelatory knowledge*, a term commonly accepted within Charismatic circles. This revelatory knowledge can be deceptive, possibly adding to God's Word through visions and/or dreams, which are taken at face value, without waiting on God to seek discernment as to their source. Many of these manifestations can be metaphysical, or may even come from an angel of light.

The "G" within the Masonic logo refers to Luciferian Gnosticism. John the beloved, in 1 John 4, warned of this Gnostic antichrist spirit, a spirit that does not believe Jesus, the Son of God, has come in the flesh.

> *Beloved, believe not every spirit, but try the spirits whether they are of God: because many false prophets are gone out into the world. Hereby know ye the Spirit of God: Every spirit that confesseth that Jesus Christ is come in the flesh is of God: And every spirit that confesseth not that Jesus Christ is come in the flesh is not of God: and this is that spirit of antichrist, whereof ye have heard that it should come; and even now already is it in the world.*
>
> (1 John 4:1-3)

In his thought-provoking, eye-opening book *Scarlet and the Beast,* Christian author and conspiracy researcher John Daniel, illustrates the Gnostic "G" within the Freemasonry logo of the square and compass.

> ...this represents the tools used by the Lodge's Great Architect (false God) to create the heavens and the earth. In reality, the letter "G" represents Gnosticism, the core doctrine of Masonry, and the Generative process (sex act).[12]

The teacher of this craft was none other than its master, Lucifer, a fallen angel. Lucifer has among his clan a third of the angelic host, who rebelled with him. They became known as demons and can take possession of the souls and bodies of those who believe Lucifer's lie. As Daniel states, a sexual doctrine is included in Masonry. It can be found among the cryptocracies; and had its early acceptance in Babylon. As Lucifer is the prince of the power of the air, is it any wonder that nothing on the media seems to "sell" without sexual overtones?

The Father's Love

The pain Jesus' torment must have caused the Father is unfathomable, beyond human comprehension. There was never a love like this---Father and son, in total harmony and agreement. The Father's most loyal, obedient, caring, loving son, Jesus, would go to earth at the Father's direction, and by His own willing act, become flesh and dwell among the vilest of humans---those whose wickedness and debauchery was indescribable. One cannot begin to understand the suffering of God the Father, knowing the pain His only begotten son would endure to destroy the works of the devil.

6

Aware of the diabolic plot by Lucifer to attempt to overthrow God's throne and establish himself as ruler over heaven and earth, the Holy Trinity[13] instituted the plan of salvation. As one, they knew it would take a substance (the blood of God) that Satan could not imitate, and could not clone. From the beginning, God foreknew the necessity of blood as the means to defeat Satan. Satan undoubtedly believed that by crucifying Jesus, his battle would be over, and he would take God's throne; but, he had no understanding of the power of the blood.

The devil didn't understand that *"...the life of the flesh is in the blood...."* (Leviticus 17:11); or, that Jesus' blood would speak, even after His death. It was Abel's blood that first spoke, crying from the ground to God about his murder by Cain. However, Jesus' *"...blood of sprinkling...speaketh better things than that of Abel."* (Hebrews 12:24). Jesus' blood speaks mercy, forgiveness, grace, salvation, healing and deliverance. Nothing will ever compare with His precious, holy blood.

The redeeming seed was first prophesied and proclaimed in the Garden by God--- the promise that a deliverer would come to destroy the evil seed.

> *And I will put enmity between thee and the woman, and between thy seed and her seed; it shall bruise thy head, and thou shalt bruise his heel.*

(Genesis 3:15)

Man's greatest power is the power of choice. It can only be exercised by an individual's own will. God has given man free will. All have been given the choice of life or death. By choosing the sacrifice prepared for us, accepting Jesus Christ as our substitutionary offering for sin, we can have life eternally. If we choose the way of Cain and the lies of Satan, it means bondage on this earth, and death followed by an eternity spent separated from God in hell with the devil and his angels.

God's plan was to be in force throughout the ages. As we have already seen, Satan has a diabolical. conspiratorial plan to unseat God and usurp His authority. He has used and will use every devious maneuver possible to ensnare men's souls for his purposes.

Ezekiel described this *created* being called Satan in Ezekiel 28. Addressed apparently to the king of Tyrus, we realize that it was not this "king" to whom Ezekiel referred to when he said, *"Thou hast been in Eden."*

> *Son of man, take up a lamentation upon the king of Tyrus, and say unto him, Thus saith the Lord GOD; Thou sealest up the sum, full of wisdom, and perfect in beauty. Thou hast been in Eden the garden of God; every precious stone was thy covering, the sardius, topaz, and the diamond, the beryl, the onyx, and the jasper, the sapphire, the emerald, and the carbuncle, and gold: the workmanship of thy tabrets and of thy pipes was prepared in thee in the day that thou wast created. Thou art the anointed cherub that covereth; and I have set thee so: thou wast upon the holy mountain of God; thou hast walked up and down in the midst of the stones of fire. Thou*

wast perfect in thy ways from the day that thou wast created, till iniquity was found in thee.

(Ezekiel 28:12-15)

Rebels

Satan's knowledge of music and its mesmerizing effect and power to captivate audiences has been a wicked ploy. Since the 1960s, entire generations have been artfully deceived into perverted sex, suicide and murder through the sense realms of sound, sight, smell, touch and taste brought about through music's effect. Our youth, as well as indulgent, ignorant adults, have fallen prey to this subtlety. The adversary, extremely cunning and beguiling, has infiltrated his beat into some churches, thereby obstructing true worship.

Rebellion in its highest form is a denial of God, turning from faith in Him to open defiance...apostasy. Satan uses cynical, bitter, proud men---unreasonable and determined to do their own thing---men who choose evil instruction and ignore God's wisdom. Judas Iscariot was only one among thousands of apostates. Some of the worst among them were men like Caiphas, Nero, Trotsky, Marx, Lenin, Weishaupt, Crowley, Arafat, Castro and Rothschild, to name but a few.

The flood that God used to purify the earth did not keep men from profane and perverse spirits. Some time after alighting from the ark, Noah fell asleep drunk. Ham saw his father in this drunken state and delighted to tell his brothers of their father's nakedness.

The Bible does not relate the act that Noah considered

deserving of a curse. No matter what the profane, perverse act was, Noah pronounced a curse on his son, Ham. As in the case of Cain, God "…made him accursed, and threatened his posterity in the seventh generation."[14]

The evil seed gained entrance into the world through Adam and Eve. Fed by wicked men, it grew until the time of Nimrod, when it knew no bounds. Then, God overthrew Babel. The evil "craft" scattered along with the people, gaining new twists, turns, gods and goddesses under a multitude of names. As their language and cultures changed, their gods' names took new form.

Ever so clever, Satan went undercover, developing secret societies to do his bidding. The occult sciences of Babel have resurfaced, prepared to ensnare additional millions into believing "the lie" and cause them to believe they are "gods." Multitudes led by extremely heinous men are blinded by Satan, who ultimately will destroy them.

Evil cryptocracies filled with men and women reprobate and independent of God, haters of Jesus, and many times their own families, have been working together to form a Utopia of their own, a Utopia bent on destroying those not in agreement with them. Their root teaching and knowledge comes from the Ancient Wisdom of Gnosticism, the mysticism of the cabala, and perverted Jewish writings from the Talmud. Deluded and deceived, the whole world lies in gloominess and darkness brought on by their fraudulent deceit.

CHAPTER TWO

NIMROD'S KINGDOM

And God saw that the wickedness of man was great in the earth, and that every imagination of the thoughts of his heart was only evil continually.

(Genesis 6:5)

Josephus relates that Shem was well versed in astronomy, understood the plan of the ages and its interpretation through the stars. It is believed Enoch instructed Shem in astrological knowledge, as it has been claimed that Enoch was given the plans for, and was architect of, the Great Pyramid.

Noah's three sons were Shem, Ham and Japheth. He cursed Ham, because Ham found his father drunk, and discovered his nakedness. The curse was visited down upon Ham's ancestry, among them, was Nimrod.

And Ham, the father of Canaan, saw the nakedness of his father, and told his two brethren without. And Shem and Japheth took a garment, and laid it upon both their shoulders, and went backward, and covered the nakedness of their father; and their faces were backward, and they saw not their father's nakedness. And Noah awoke from his wine, and knew what his younger son had done unto him. And he said, Cursed be Canaan; a servant of servants shall he be

unto his brethren.   And he said, Blessed be
the Lord God of Shem; and Canaan shall be
his servant.

(Genesis 9:22-26)

According to Josephus, Shem outlived Abraham by thirty-three years.   He lived during Nimrod's reign and was in direct opposition to Nimrod, standing for righteousness, as did Abraham.   It was Shem who was credited for destroying Nimrod (also known as Tammuz, and countless other names).[15, 16, 17]   After the flood, Shem, Ham and Japheth scattered and through their progeny repopulated the earth.

Ham fathered the Assyrians, Babylonians, Canaanites, Cushites, Egyptians, Ethiopians and Libyans. Cush, Ham's grandson, fathered Nimrod. Nimrod ruled these same areas with force and cunning. He was decidedly more wicked than his accursed ancestry. Nimrod was a sinister, tyrannical despot, menacing the people under his rule. However, even his deeds will be surpassed by the coming Antichrist, whose body after he's slain, will be possessed by Satan himself.

Named for one of Ham's grandsons, the history of the nation of Canaan is rather obscure. Known because of Joshua's conquest, the Lord commanded Joshua and the Israelites to conquer it, undoubtedly because of the despicable religious practices within its borders. The region of Canaan included the Hivites, Girgashites, Amorites, Hittites, Perrizites, Jebusites, as well as Canaanites.

These people practiced all manner of sexual depravation and participated in sexual fertility rites.

Contrary to some teaching which denigrates the black race, Ham's curse came because he carried evil seeds of rebellion, idolatry, witchcraft; and, most likely, immoral acts, as alluded to in the terminology used in Genesis 9:24. His iniquitous heritage came to fruition through Nimrod; and, after the Babel dispersion, traversed the world, sparking false religions, cults and secret societies.

Nimrod's Domain

Nimrod combined church and state by a government of force over the people under his control. Nimrod's "religion" included incest, like the relationship he had with his wife/mother, Semiramis, also known as Astarte, et al. His seditious plans were futuristic as well and have cunningly been carried out through his seed and their evil associates hoodwinking men of all nations into "Nimrodian" (Luciferian-dictated) doctrines down through the centuries.

Intimidated and manipulated by Nimrod, the people in his realm feared the Lord would bring another flood upon them. Despite God's promise to the contrary, and prodded on by Nimrod, the people rebelled at the Lord's command to establish individual townships (colonies) and constructed the Tower of Babel instead.

> Nimrod excited them to…contempt of God… the multitudes were very ready to follow the determination of Nimrod and to esteem it a place of cowardice to submit to God; and they built a tower….[18]

> Actually, the purpose of the tower was to provide a common religious center as a

rallying point, lest the people be scattered. The builders of the tower were in open defiance of God's command. [19,]

Those in Nimrod's domain were more interested in their wicked sexual practices than in the tower itself. From this evil edifice emerged a religious creed established by Nimrod and Semiramis, consisting of gods and goddesses, priests and priestesses, which offered animal and human sacrifices upon their altars. Towers where these blasphemous rites were practiced were scattered throughout the entire kingdom.

The tower, built in pyramid form, was considered the grandest of all. Highly regarded by the people for its height and dedication to their worship, this massive tower loomed high above the rest, and was centered in the City of Babylon.

Babylon became the seat of Nimrod's empire. It contained large avenues, tall, magnificent buildings and may similar towers, known as ziggurats. Worship was dedicated to Nimrod, Semiramis, and a multitude of gods and goddesses, which Nimrod was supposedly to have sired, and which Semiramis supposedly bore.

Knowledge received by the people who worshipped in these ziggurats was obtained through contact with demons. The people were also encouraged to counsel with "stargazers," who read stars for daily guidance, as do present-day astrologers. Priests and priestesses engaged in sexual orgies and sacrifices, both with animals and humans, "servicing" their gods.

Among the demonically inspired, words we believe

to mean one thing meant quite the opposite to them. We consider a virgin one who has abstained from sexual practices and remains pure until marriage. A virgin in Nimrod's satanic culture was not considered as such unless she had had intercourse with a priest. A non-virgin was called a virgin. This "doublespeak" is still used among cryptocracies. They say one thing when they mean something entirely different.

> It was thought that sacred and ritual sex cleansed and purified, therefore the term "virgin" was used, though its meaning is obviously far different than that envisioned by Christians.[20]

Thor Heyerdahl, as revealed in his two books, *Kon Tiki* and *Ra,* replicated boats made of materials from the area controlled by Nimrod. He believed it possible to sail these frail craft to South America and the islands, which he did. His findings proved that people from the Middle East could journey to and possibly establish the ancient pyramids found among the tribes of Mexico, Central and South America, and the strange stone formations found on Easter Island. Pyramid-type edifices found in those countries and their purposes of false worship are markedly similar to the Tower of Babel and the towers in and around the nations Nimrod ruled.

This type of travel at the time of the destruction of the Tower of Babel could explain why Catholic Jesuits, who traveled into the Far East were greatly surprised when they saw statues of a mother holding a child, like the Catholic rendition of Mary and Jesus. These idols had been established long before the area was evangelized by the Catholics.

That the birth of the Great Deliverer was to be miraculous, was widely known long before the Christian era. For centuries... Buddhist priests had a tradition that a *Virgin* was to bring forth a child to bless the world. That this tradition came from no Popish or Christian source, is evident from the surprise felt and expressed by the Jesuit missionaries, when they first entered Thibet and China and...found a mother and a child worshipped as at home, but that mother worshipped under a character ...corresponding with...their... Madonna...the *Virgin* Mother.of God, and... in regions where they could not find the least trace of either the name or history of our Lord Jesus Christ having ever been known.[21]

There are indications that when God confused the languages and the peoples scattered, their idolatrous and incestuous worship followed them. As they developed their own particular culture, the names of their gods and goddesses changed, as did their language.

Ancient Wisdom is gaining international acceptance. This wisdom is nothing more than the knowledge of good and evil, which ensnared Adam and Eve. Like them, the deceived are being subtly captivated and seduced. Spawned by world apostasy, this "wisdom" is reaching a climax, about to overtake the present generation. Evidence of it is all about us.

In many cities, buildings and/or objects are shaped like pyramids, and/or obelisks. The obelisk was designed among the degenerate to imitate a male phallus. The male phallus and female womb are objects of worship in secret societies, especially within Freemasonry. Obelisk examples are the Washington Monument, another on the property near the Supreme Court Building in Israel, and another outside St. Peter's Basilica in Rome.

To the willfully ignorant and rebellious, or unlearned and unbelieving, these false cultish edifices seem inconsequential; however, wisdom is known of her children, and God would have us know the truth of these false concepts, which were initiated by Satan himself..

Among religious superstitions practiced in Nimrod's kingdom, and a part of today's same religious practices, are these:

Abortion	Infanticide
Alcohol abuse	Karma
Altered states of consciousness	Levitation
Animism	Meditation
Astral travel	Mystery teachings and initiations
Astrology	Nature worship (sun, moon, earth, etc.)
Chants	Necromancy
Demonic healing	Occult symbolism
Divination	Oracular magic
Doctrine that man is god	Palmistry
Drug Abuse	Personal transformation (rebirth)
Fire worship	Prosperity from gods doctrine
Gemology	Psychic/Mind powers
Goddess worship	Reincarnation
Herbology	Shamanism
Hypotism	Self-love (narcissism)
Idolatry	Sex magic (magick)
Incense	Tarot card reading
	Visualization[22]

Resurgence of pyramid designs coupled with an increase in idolatry and superstition is an indication of the resurrection of Nimrod's kingdom…a type and shadow of the Antichrist kingdom to come. The Ancient Mysteries with cabala mysticism have widely gained acceptance in a corrupt society, bent on destruction.

CHAPTER THREE

A ONE WORLD CHURCH

Let no man deceive you by any means: for that day shall not come, except there come a falling away first, and that man of sin be revealed, the son of perdition.

(2 Thessalonians 2:3)

In ancient Babylon, Semiramis was worshipped as a fertility goddess. She was known as the "Mother of God," or "Mother of Gods;" and, the deceived believed she was responsible for the birth of all pagan gods through her son, Nimrod. As "Queen of Heaven," she "...led a licentious life, and gave birth to many illegitimate children. Yet, the people grew to worship her as the "Holy Virgin."

The image of mother with a child in her arms was so firmly entrenched in the pagan mind that by the time Christianity appeared on the scene, these statues and paintings were merely renamed and worshiped as the Virgin Mary with her god-incarnate son, Jesus. Thus, the pagan mother and child entered Christianity as the Roman Catholic worship of Mary with the infant Jesus.

First established in Babylon, where Nimrod was adored and lauded, his mother soon succeeded him in worship and was heartily acclaimed by the masses. When Nimrod died, she elevated her own position as a so-called divine deity. The image of a mother with child was accepted long before the advent of Jesus' birth, and its worship spread throughout the then known world.

Semiramis has an undetermined number of other names, but all can be found to come from the same Babylonian religious cult. As "Queen of Heaven," she was given the following "goddess" names in Greece: Aphrodite, Artemis, Athena, Demeter, Gaea (Gaia), Herea, Hestia and Rhea. In Rome, she was known as: Venus, Diana, Minerva, Ceres, Terra, Juno, Vesta and Ops.[23]

Under God's direction, Jeremiah, the prophet, boldly decried the worship of the queen of heaven.

> *The children gather wood, and the fathers kindle the fire, and the women knead their dough, to make cakes to the queen of heaven, and to pour out drink offerings unto other gods, that they may provoke me to anger.*

> (Jeremiah 7:18)

In the Islamic faith, she is known as Ishtar, which means star. This is the same goddess known as Astarte of Babylon, or Isis of Egypt. Mary is sometimes called, "Our Lady of Fatima," and worshipped not only by Catholics, but Hindus as well. Those individuals who are unlearned or blinded in the things of the living God, fall prey to mythology and its many gods, all of which are nothing more than a maneuver of Satan to deceive the masses and cause them to turn from the Lord.

The lie of Eden stated in Genesis 3:5, *"...and ye shall be as gods, knowing good and evil,"* was subtly fed to the naive, who easily bought into it. Thus, many became "gods" and "goddesses," practicing, as history records, "... temple prostitution, human sacrifice, infanticide, abortion and gruesome barbarism...."[24]

Nor was it confined to the pagans. The scripturally ignorant began to worship idols as paganism became "wedded" to the Roman Catholic Church. This was accomplished during the reign of Constantine the Great, an early Roman emperor. The union of church and state served Constantine's purpose well in building his empirical kingdom.

Prevalent within false religions to the present time, tt has taken root in secular humanism, out of which Nazism evolved. It is promoted subtly through success motivational seminars, whose psychological ploys tell people they can "do it" themselves by positive thinking and "right" attitudes; whereas, some 12-step programs encourage belief in a higher-power, but not necessarily the power of Almighty God. These are but New Age self-governing ideologies, which assist the New Age spiritual movement in building its One World Church under Antichrist.

Strange Phenomena

False religion embraces a trinity in keeping with its "copycat" status; i.e., Satan, an antitype of God; Lucifer, an antitype of the Holy Spirit (through worldwide Masonic influence); the Antichrist (or son of perdition), an antitype of the Son of God, Jesus Christ. Their version includes the mother goddess, they now called Mary. She, of course, is but a reproduction of the Babylonian Semiramis. "Mary's" ghostlike appearances to multitudes produce what seem to be miraculous healings and strange phenomena, such as talking heads, weeping and bleeding statues, etc. This Mary quite often appears as the "Lady of Fatima."

Protestant believers would be wise to discern some of the unusual manifestations found in some congregations.

Satan is not above unusual, powerful manifestations to *"...deceive the very elect."* (Matthew 24:24) Statues that bleed or cry (stigmata) are common sights the gullible and deceived take to be truly supernatural. These stigmata are supernatural all right, but, from demonic sources.

Many tricks of Satan and his demonized hordes fool the naive into believing these ghostlike appearances and supernatural manifestations are miracles from God. In their delusion, they believe these statues and/or medals can answer prayer; i.e., Saint Elmo supposedly protects ships at sea, and Saint Christopher medals are worn as a talisman to protect travelers.

Satan will gladly make things appear as though prayer has been answered by these dead saints if it will ensnare a soul. If Satan can trap a soul into believing a statue of wood or stone, or a pendant cast in metal can answer prayer, he has fully succeeded in his deceit and gained converts to his illusions. Of course, those who aren't deceived and manufacture them, gladly take in "the loot" from these items.

False Prophet

Some believe the false prophet will come from within the Catholic Church--- possibly a future pope---and direct the world through signs and wonders to worship the Antichrist. Others believe the pope himself will be the Antichrist; however, this is unlikely. There are three strong possibilities at present of individuals who fit the description of the Antichrist, and none of them is the pope.

And upon her forehead was a name written, MYSTERY, BABYLON THE GREAT,

THE MOTHER OF HARLOTS AND ABOMINATIONS OF THE EARTH.

(Revelation 17:5)

There is only one church known as the "mother" church, and that is Catholicism. Her "harlot" churches include denominations which have a measure of truth, but incorporate unbiblical doctrines. She is regaining many who have left her ranks in spite of the sexual perversion recently uncovered within many of her parishes.

Scripture says the false prophet will have miraculous power. Wherever there is truth, Satan is lurking in the shadows with his counterfeits. Charismatics would be wise to use discernment concerning unusual manifestations, inasmuch as supernatural signs follow that movement. These signs will become more and more prevalent as the day of the Lord approaches.

Other strange practices in church services such as snake handling, or so-called believers barking like dogs, or eruptions of raucous laughter, which interrupt genuine worship and over shadow God's Word, negate the message of the cross, bring reproach upon God and the church; and usually end in ruin with no genuine repentance on the part of those who accept such manifestations. All these have served the purpose of bringing pleasure to Satan, and undermining truth.

Souls who follow "signs" can easily be captivated by the miraculous. It matters not the church or denomination. Jesus warned, *"A wicked and adulterous generation seeketh after a sign...."* (Matthew 16:4) Those attracted to pagan rites, strange manifestations and symbolism, and lying

signs and wonders will find themselves totally deceived by
the second beast of Revelation if they continue to follow
unscriptural practices.

> *And I beheld another beast coming up out of
> the earth; and he had two horns like a lamb,
> and he spake as a dragon. And he exerciseth
> all the power of the first beast before him,
> and causeth the earth and them which dwell
> therein to worship the first beast, whose
> deadly wound was healed. And he doeth
> great wonders, so that he maketh fire come
> down from heaven on the earth in the sight
> of men....*

(Revelation 13:11-13)

The Israelites provoked the Lord by idol worship.
How much more have the children of God provoked Him
today by following every sign, wind of doctrine, myth, old
wives' tale, or by bowing down to graven images and/or
the queen of heaven under the guise of religion? As long
as they had their wants met, they didn't care whether or not
they obeyed God. The same can be said of the lukewarm
Laodicean Church of this age.

> *But we will certainly do whatsoever thing
> goeth forth out of our own mouth, to burn
> incense unto the queen of heaven, and to
> pour out drink offerings unto her, as we
> have done, we, and our fathers, our kings,
> and our princes, in the cities of Judah, and
> in the streets of Jerusalem: for then had we
> plenty of victuals, and were well, and saw no
> evil. But since we left off to burn incense to*

the queen of heaven, and to pour out drink
offerings unto her, we have wanted all things,
and have been consumed by the sword and by
the famine.

(Jeremiah 44:17-18)

Ignorance of the devil and his devices (such as the above manifestations) is no excuse. God gives man every opportunity to repent. Evil seeds sown do bear fruit. Man has been given the power of choice. Wrong choices and rebellion toward God lead men straight into Satan's lair, opening their minds to demonic control and possession.

Sacrilege

Illuminists have strong ties with each other as blood brothers through oaths taken in clandestine meetings. They blasphemously declare Lucifer, a fallen angel, as Jesus' brother. Worldwide church councils, organized by an Illuminist trio for the purpose of gathering the world under one "faith" are sinister and fiendish, having roots in the worship of Lucifer; and intent on building a One World Church, which will deny the Lord as God come in the flesh, His sacrificial death, burial and resurrection,.

> ...the Rockefellers, the Rothschilds, and J. P. Morgan, working with the Unitarians and Freemasons created the Federal Council of Churches of Christ, the National Council of Churches, and the World Council of Churches.[25]

All families of the Illuminati are deeply involved in witchcraft and occult practices. Along with many of our government leaders, they take part in Bohemian Grove rites where they participate in ceremonies held near a huge statue of an owl, which some call "Moloch." Moloch, or Molech, is also known as Baal. The children of Israel, when in idolatry, offered their children to the fiery ovens of this idol. It is quite possible, because many government and church officials are involved in the Bohemian Grove rites to Moloch, that the abortion laws are an attempt to appease this same evil entity.

Cryptocracies use secret hand signals and other identifying signs, in this way they recognize others of mutual affiliation. Magic and sacrilegious rites are performed in clandestine meetings, often presided over by an adept.

An adept is "one who shows knowledge, skill or aptitude in magic."[26] Among the Illuminist families are those whose knowledge is spiritual, while the knowledge of others is financial. Ranked among the spiritual is the Collins' family.

> The year is 1955, and all the Mother-of-Darkness level families are attending this ritual...The Grande Dame on the throne is called Queen Mother and she is a Collins... Seven children from generational Satanic families...dressed in white are presented to the Queen Mother Collins...they lay prostrate and worship her...[She]...would then move her scepter...up and down...She would strike the scepter to show approval of a child candidate...after approving the candidates, 7 other children were then sacrificed and the blood of the dead child...used to write the

approved child's name on parchment using a quill.

Within the Illuminati rituals, they emphasize that the 13th bloodline is that they are the seed of Satan. As their secret story goes, they are the direct descendants of Jesus' spiritual brother, Lucifer.[27]

Royal Intrigue

Royal European families of Merovingian descent are among the extremely wealthy elitists who have chosen to rule the world under Lucifer's direction. These families would have the world believe they are direct descendents of Jesus Christ and Mary Magdalene. Lying propaganda about Mary Magdalene and Jesus has been deliberately distributed to deceive the unwary. Many have fallen prey to these deceptions, believing the blasphemous works of *The Last Temptation of Christ, Jesus Christ Superstar, The Da Vinci Code,* and other profane works.

In recent months, these deceivers claimed to have found the graves of Mary Magdalene, Jesus and an imaginary body of Jesus. Scripture contradicts this, saying, Joseph of Arimathea *"...went unto Pilate, and begged the body of Jesus. And he took it down, and wrapped it in linen, and laid it in a sepulcher that was hewn in stone, wherein never man before was laid."* (Luke 23:52-53).

Jesus is alive; He rose from the dead. Without the resurrection, Christianity would be senseless. Every believer knows He lives! The fact of the resurrection sets the Christian's faith apart from all other faiths.

This Magdalene/Christ deception serves the purpose

of establishing the One World Church of Revelation 17. It implements their plans to install Antichrist as king of Jerusalem, claiming his descent from King David.

> However, it is clear that in recent history, the various nodes of power in the world have been congealed into one super World Order. This congealing has been the goal of the Merovingian dynasty for many centuries. They saw the ultimate fulfillment of this primarily through the British Empire, secret societies, and socialism. They have worked and interbred with other powerful bloodlines such as Nimrod's, the leadership of Mystery Religions, the Tribe of Benjamin, the Tribe of Dan, the Scythians, the Roman Aristocracy and Roman Caesars and Black Venetian Nobility (Guelphs). They are the House of David. The prominent bloodlines which are connected to witchcraft and the Mystery Religions.[28]

Fritz Springmeier relates that British Israelism is not new, but has long been the belief of those in the British Commonwealth. Most of our U.S. presidents are related to England's monarchy. There is much available data regarding the intermarriages of royalty and their connections with our presidents and shared interaction with cryptocracies

Inasmuch as the Jewish people believe their Messiah has to be a descendant of King David, knowledge of the British lineage will play a big part in their acceptance of the Antichrist, should he be from Britain. The Brits do claim descent from King David; and, this is entirely possible, as Jeremiah 33:17 states: *"For thus saith the Lord; David shall never want a man to sit upon the throne of the house of Israel...."*

History appears to confirm their claim, as Queen Elizabeth's lineage chart traces her ancestry back to the tribe of Judah. However, there are deep occult practices and apostasy within British royalty. This occultism could have developed through King Solomon and his witchcraft-oriented wives...not King David. Whatever happens, it is certain the British Commonwealth has played a huge part in the development of the State of Israel, however deceitful their plans may have been.

The Royal family appears outwardly Christian through their affiliation with the Anglican Church/Church of England. However, they are reported to be involved in various forms of witchcraft and occultism and have strong connections with the Illuminati. Their lives reveal nothing of the life of Christ, or the work of the Cross; rather, their philanthropies are but good works, pretentious at most.

All religions will soon unite under one banner, forming the One World Church. It quite possibly is Catholicism. Whatever it is, it will be under a pretense of peace and tolerance, and will exclude the finished work of the cross and the shed blood of the Lord, and attract those who have fallen prey to Satan's deception.

CHAPTER FOUR

ALTERED TEXTS

But there were false prophets also among the people, even as there shall be false teachers among you, who privily shall bring in damnable heresies, even denying the Lord that bought them, and bring upon themselves swift destruction.

(2 Peter 2:1)

Masons, counted among the bloodlines of the Illuminati, introduced well-known cults. The two most prominent were Charles Taze Russell, leader of Jehovah's Witnesses; and, Joseph Smith and Brigham Young, who founded the Mormon Church, otherwise known as the Church of Jesus Christ of Latter Day Saints. Joseph Smith was believed to have been murdered because he integrated Masonic teachings into Mormonism, revealing Masonic secrets.

Another cultist is Rick Warren, whose books, *The Purpose Driven Life,* and *The Purpose Driven Church,* subtly lead away from the work of the cross and into New Age humanistic/hedonistic teaching. These self-serving ideals are much the same that enticed Hitler's "Christian" followers into believing his lie, and entering into the Third Reich.

In many instances the church remained silent in the face of Nazi outrages. In other cases, the church actively aided and supported the

Nazis. In still other cases, the church failed to counter erroneous teachings that eventually led to easy acceptance of Nazi doctrine.[29]

Warren, who in recent years has been recognized internationally and had the somewhat ignominious achievement of speaking before the United Nations sharing his "peace" plan, was mentored by Robert Schuller, a 33-degree Mason, who drew upon the teachings of psychologist Carl Jung and New Age philosopher Jerry Jampolsky. Warren's books contain New Age doctrine, and his teachings are recognized by the New Age Movement as a means to unify the church world. His teaching has reached into entire communities and countries, such as Rowanda. As a preacher, he has combined church and state including Hillary Clinton and Barack Obama as speakers from his Saddleback Church platform. Millions are being "hoodwinked" by the psychological babble within his books, unable to distinguish truth from error.

Robert Schuller, Warren's mentor, taught at the Unity School. Although Schuller knew that Luciferian initiations and witchcraft were practiced there, he didn't object, nor did he hesitate to teach his church growth techniques---the same ones he taught to Warren, and Warren has used to advantage.

Interestingly, a man who was part of the Unity School hierarchy, and came to Christ told me that the school secretly conducted Luciferian initiations and that Robert Schuller, 33° Mason, and leading Protestant clergyman knew all about Luciferian initiations being conducted there, yet Schuller went ahead and taught his principles of church growth to Unity School. They call the school Unity School of Christianity, but a more accurate name would be Unity School of Witchcraft. Many witches have in fact been associated with the Unity Church and are closely working with it to secretly destroy Christianity.[30]

Partial financial backing for Warren is received from none other than Rupert Murdock. Murdock (also spelled Murdoch) controls much of our media: radio, television and several newspapers. His holdings include FOX News, and surprisingly for an Illuminist "Jew" and Communist sympathizer, a Christian publication company. Murdock made the following comments about his media worldwide outreach:

> Our reach is unmatched around the world. We're reaching people from the moment they wake up until they fall asleep. We give them their morning weather and traffic reports through our television outlets around the world. We enlighten and entertain them with such newspapers as *The New York Post* and *The Times* (of London) as they have breakfast, or take the train to work. We update their stock prices and give them the world's biggest news stories every day through such news channels as FOX or Sky News...And when they get home in the evening we're there to entertain them with compelling first-run entertainment on FOX or the day's biggest game on our broadcast, satellite and

cable networks. Before going to bed, we give them the latest news, and then they crawl into bed with one of our best-selling novels from Harper-Collins. (Rupert Murdoch, News Corporation, 1999 Annual Report).[31]

The term "old fox" is a title often given to homosexuals. Jesus used it in reference to King Herod, who lived a profane lifestyle. (Luke 13:32) Most within the Illuminati are homosexual or bisexual. With that in mind, it will be interesting to see where FOX News will take the public with their news and views. Many think them conservative, but that is not necessarily true.

> Some say the word and name of 'Fox' has hidden cabalistic significance. Numerologically, the letters F-O-X in the English alphabet equal the sum of 666. Jesus once called Israel's King Herod, a murderous scheming man who embraced magic, 'That old fox'. Fox television network is owned by Rupert Murdock, an ardent Zionist....[32]

Andrew Carrington Hitchcock in his book, *The Synagogue of Satan,* writes concerning Zionists:

> Regretably, this Luciferian Cabal...is supported by over eighteen million people around the globe, who call themselves "Jews." Some of these people, a great many, are fanatical in their support of the Synagogue of Satan. They go by the name, "Zionists." Others provide the Cabal with only token, often nominal, support."[33]

We need to discern the spirit of antichrist; which denies Jesus Christ is the Son of God, who came to earth in the flesh to redeem mankind; anyone who does not accept that fact, be they Jew or Gentile, has an antichrist spirit. Why, then, would a non-Messianic Communist sympathizer, Illuminist Jew be interested in controlling a Christian bookstore? Or, have controlling interests in a Christian publishing company?

When you read in the 2001 annual report of the Rupert Murdock Corporation for 2001, you will find in the holdings section Harper-Collins Publishing. You then have to look elsewhere to see what they own. When you do, you find a name familiar to most Christians: Zondervan, the largest Bible publisher in the world.[34]

Blasphemy

To accomplish the goals of the Illuminati's One World Government, the populace must be made to believe that globalism is in their best interest. The best way to do this is through the media and the distribution of mass propaganda, weaning the people from the truth.

Of interest to the reader might be the knowledge that Murdock has been called by Mike Royco, a Chicago columnist, the media's prince of darkness. This may be because Murdock not only has the copyright for the NIV, but also for Hustler magazine. The rights to the New International Bible Version include all the printing rights. The NIV has more sales than any other version worldwide. Another surprising fact is that Murdock also has the copyright to another corrupted Bible version, the Amplified Bible, in which many faithfully put their trust. Hopefully, this information will cause many to take a serious look at what is being taught from these versions and compare the teaching from them with the King James Version.

Harper-Collins Publishing, under the financial umbrella of Murdock, controls Family Christian Bookstores. Zondervan and Family Christian Bookstores have become quite liberal in their selection of products. Few, who frequent the bookstores' establishment realize the extent to which they are purchasing works framed to deceive. Truth that has been watered down, or adulterated to appease the liberal, lukewarm believer, can lead to apostasy. Apostasy stems from lack of knowledge of the Word of God. This lack will result in disobedience, unbelief, and, finally, if left unchecked, total denial of faith in God. As Hosea said: *"My people are destroyed for lack of knowledge...."* (Hosea 6:3)

Not only have believers been, as one writer puts it, "weaned" from the truth, they have been inundated with a multiplicity of faulty Bible translations, many designed for the express purpose of seducing the believer from true faith, and the message of the cross.

This is not to say a believer cannot be blessed by other versions; but, to make them aware they may have an inaccurate, adulterated text. It is no secret that the Holy Spirit can minister life to any one even with the smallest portion of God's Word. We are in no way attempting to diminish the grace of God in using whatever means He chooses to reveal Himself to souls, rather to alert them to the corruption of some texts.

Below is a small example of diluted and/or adulterated texts. Wescott and Hort's Bible translations are considered corrupted, taken from corrupted earlier texts, and then translated into Greek. For a better understanding of their source, we must take a look at the individuals themselves, those men who translated this sullied text. Who, we must ask, were Wescott and Hort? First of all, they were not Christian by Biblical definition. And, secondly, what were their motives and the impetus for their actions? Who influenced them?

Wescott and Hort in their youth were two Greek students at Oxford College. Oxford is the college where Cecil Rhodes willed money for scholarships to young people thought worthy to follow in his footsteps. (Rhodes' investments were initially financed by Rothschild…more about him in Chapter 11.) Wescott and Hort "…compiled a Greek text from what they claimed to be 'the most reliable' manuscripts available at the time."[35]

> Wescott and Hort's biggest influence was Madam Blavatsky. Ask any student of the occult who she is. She was the most powerful witch ever to live, and founded New Age theology. She met with and mentored both Wescott and Hort personally. They attended séances she held.
>
> As a result of her influence, Wescott and Hort went on to establish an organization known as the "ghostly ghouls," which practiced more "dialogue with the dead" (demons), and homosexuality.[36]

The text they compiled furthered acceptance of the newer erroneous versions in use today. There has been such an influx of contaminated texts, it is vitally necessary for the believer to seek the Lord as to the truth of whatever they read, or believe to be gospel.

> *For I testify unto every man that heareth the words of the prophecy of this book, If any man shall add unto these things, God shall add unto him the plagues that are written in this book: And if any man shall take away from the words of the book of this prophecy, God shall take away his part out of the book of life, and out of the holy city, and from the things which are written in this book.*

(Revelation 22:18-19)

One seriously altered text is the New International Version, which reportedly contains 65,000 omissions and 25,000 critical errors. It has been compared by Pastor Lee Garrett with the original bible issued by Watchtower of the Jehovah's Witness cult. Pastor Garrett discovered:

> EVERY heretical change made in the 1922 Jehovah's Witness version of scripture was DUPLICATED in today's New International Version, published by Zondervan. Les went on to discover hundreds of more changes and omissions in the NIV. Many, if not most pertained to essential Christian doctrine: the virgin birth, the Deity of Christ and his resurrection.[37]

The reader will recall that the Jehovah's Witness cult originated under the tuteledge of Charles Taze Russell, who was of Illuminist bloodlines. Illuminists are known to worship Lucifer, otherwise known as Satan. The Witnesses have as their doctrinal "bible" a volume called *The New*

World Translation.

If this were the only faulty Bible translation, there might not be as much deception within the church; however, the Lockman Foundation's translator, Dr. Frank Logsdon, told of corruption in another well-known version. His work of translation on the New American Standard Bible was taken from the texts of Wescott and Hort. When he discovered their manuscript to be erroneous, he attempted to stop its public distribution.

> ...before his death, Dr. Logsdon recants and with great disgrace and dismay in his voice, disavowing the entire NASV as being an awful corruption of God's word. He said he was proud of his work until he discovered the text he had worked from those many years was corrupt to the core.[38]

Much to Logsdon's sorrow, the publisher, Lockman Foundation, refused to remove the corrupted texts from distribution.

Many of the beloved Bibles in use today have been extremely corrupted, translated by Wescott and Hort, who, as stated before, were swayed by the occult during the years they translated the Bible. The most solid version today is still the Authorized King James Version, although it is being "debunked" by New Age propaganda, apparently with good success. Another good, easier to read version, is the New King James Version.

It would be unrealistic not to consider using other texts for deeper understanding and comparison of scripture verses. However, with few exceptions, other texts omit important scriptures such as those which refer to Jesus' blood, the cross, or the resurrection…the foundations of our faith.

> *If the foundations be destroyed, what can the righteous do?*

> (Psalm 11:3)

Rev. Charles Salliby also made a comparison between the New International Version and the King James Version. There are so many omissions within the NIV it would take pages upon pages to note them. However, this one small example should be sufficient for the individual who sincerely wants the truth:

The name "Jesus" was removed forty-six times in the NIV. Here is one very sad example:

> (KJV) "Then charged he his disciples that they should tell no man that he was Jesus the Christ."

> (NIV) "Then he warned his disciples not to tell anyone that he was the Christ."

> This is certainly a pitiful omission since this is the only place in the four Gospels where Christ called Himself "Jesus." The name Jesus means "Jehovah is Salvation" Whom Christ in this verse acknowledged Himself to be. Therefore…the designs against Him appear to be self evident.[39]

This example is minute compared to the multiplied changes within many modern Bibles. Satan was the first to alter God's Word in Eden. He hasn't changed his tactics.

...much of what is wrong with modern Bibles can be traced back to the ancient Gnostics who prefigured the Antichrist. Thus, the Gnostics, Origen, Constantine, Wescott, Hort, Antichrist and many lesser names between are synonymous. They all contributed to a "Satanic Masterpiece."

---First, the Gnostics and Origen blended the Scriptures with the pagan's view of Christ.

---Then, Constantine, with the aid of these Scriptures, blended Christianity with paganism.

---Currently, with these same Scriptures, numerous Church leaders and theologians, under the delusion of Wescott and Hort, are blending Protestantism with Catholicism.

---Which, next, will be blended with every other religion.

---And then, finally, with the pagan world, in a One World Empire under a One World Emperor.[40]

Most believers are unaware of what Gnosticism is. According to Dr. Larry Spargimino, Ph.D.,

Gnosticism (from the Greek word *gnosis*, meaning "knowledge" was an ancient religious movement that began in the centuries before Christ, and flourished during the second and third centuries A.D. It was generally syncretistic (accommodating of many religious, hence tolerant of a diversity of views). Its main teaching is that human beings are divine souls trapped in a physical world created by an imperfect deity, the demiurge, who was incorrectly identified with the God of Abraham.[41]

Gnosticism incorporates and tolerates all religions, including those which do not believe that Jesus Christ is Lord. It has generated the New Age ecumenical movement...the religious movement, whose doctrine will be honored by the Antichrist.

Gnosticism has influenced literature (William Blake), philosophy (Schopenhauer), esoterists (Madame Blavatsky, Albert Pike) and psychiatry (Carl Jung). Others who were heavily influenced by this philosophical outlook are Aleister Crowley, Albert Camus, the "hippie" poet Allen Ginsberg, and Dan Brown, author of *The Da Vinci Code*.[42]

It is the concept ushering in the emergent church, the seeker friendly church, and contemplative spirituality; all, of which lead the believer away from the blood, the cross and the resurrection into "psycho babble", humanism, hedonism, metaphysics, etc.

It is no wonder Babylon was called the "Mother of Harlots." So many denominations with their "pet" doctrines have bits and pieces of truth, which add to or take away from the accepted Word of God, which has been proven to be 90% accurate...the King James Version.

CHAPTER FIVE

DANGEROUS DOCTRINES

Now the Spirit speaketh expressly, that in the latter times some shall depart from the faith, giving heed to seducing spirits, and doctrines of devils;

(1Timothy 4:1)

Doctrines that appear good, when examined under the scrutiny of the true Word of God. may prove extremely corrupt. If accepted, these false doctrines draw believers into deception, bondage and unbelief. Deceptive doctrines can lead to apostasy. The term, "apostasy", which means falling away from the faith, reveals that it is possible for one once a believer to turn away from God and fall into unbelief, and sometimes gross darkness. One such doctrine is that of once saved always saved and is based on the following scripture.

And I give unto them eternal life; and they shall never perish, neither shall any man pluck them out of my hand.

(John 10:28)

Jude in his epistle makes it clear there is a possibility of losing one's salvation and coming under God's judgment. Since angels were cast into darkness and everlasting chains because of leaving their first estate, how can one who falls into unbelief and tramples that worthy blood of Jesus underfoot, hope to escape the judgment of God and fires of Hell? It is indeed *"...a fearful thing to fall into the hands of the living God."* (Hebrews 10:31)   Apostasy, as mentioned before, happens as a result of unbelief, the same thing for which the unbelieving Israelites were destroyed in the wilderness.

> *I will therefore put you in remembrance, though ye once knew this, how that the Lord, having saved the people out of the land of Egypt, afterward destroyed them that believed not. And the angels which kept not their first estate, but left their own habitation, he hath reserved in everlasting chains under darkness unto the judgment of the great day.*

> (Jude 1:5-6)

The overall council of God's Word shows men can of their own volition deny God and serve Satan. Becoming apostate by an act of their own will and because of unbelief, their names can be blotted out of the Lamb's Book of Life.

> *And if any man shall take away from the words of the book of this prophecy, God shall take away his part out of the book of life, and out of the holy city, and from the things which are written in this book.*

> (Revelation 22:18-19)

God will do everything possible to reclaim a fallen believer, but the individual has the power of choice, and can decide to serve God or turn from the faith. This is not a subject to be taken lightly. Habitual, deliberate, disobedience to God's Word will ultimately lead to destruction. It is much better to follow the Lord whatever the cost, than presume to be safe while living in open sin and rebellion.

Demonic Theologies

We cannot discuss the One World Church (New Age Movement) without mentioning another monstrous doctrine under many names. This doctrine of devils set in motion the Holocaust and has brought extreme suffering to God-fearing Jews and Gentiles, and is subtly resurfacing. Conceived through allegorical teaching, it is known under different titles such as Dominion theology, Kingdom Now theology, Reconstructionist theology and Replacement theology. These doctrinal positions claim the church has replaced Israel.

> Generally, Reconstructionism seeks to replace democracy with a theocratic elite that would govern by imposing their interpretation of "Biblical Law." Reconstructionism would eliminate not only democracy but many of its manifestations, such as labor unions, civil rights laws, and public schools. Women would be generally relegated to hearth and home. Insufficiently Christian men would be denied citizenship, perhaps executed. So severe is this theocracy that it would extend capital punishment beyond such crimes as kidnapping, rape, and murder to include, among other things, blasphemy, heresy, adultery, and homosexuality.[43]

The believer is not under the Law, nor obligated to adhere to the laws of the Old Testament, with the exception of the 10 Commandments, which were not ceremonial laws. There are some things in which we are encouraged to participate. For instance, the observance of the Sabbath. The Sabbath is a day of rest---for God Himself rested on the seventh day; but, we are not legally bound by its observance. This day of rest was instituted before the Law was given to Moses; and, a day of rest is beneficial for our physical bodies. In addition, some dietary laws, such as omission of certain unclean animals, which can be toxic to the body, are beneficial as well. These suggested limitations are for our health, but not requirements for the New Testament believer. To bring society under this type of legal jurisdiction would bring forth slavery. We are called to liberty, not slavery.

> Reconstructionism is a theology…which proposes that contemporary application of the laws of Old Testament Israel, or "Biblical Law," is the basis for reconstructing society toward the Kingdom of God on earth.[44]

Those teaching Kingdom Now principles believe they are preparing the "kingdom" to present back to Jesus. This is a doctrine of works. Jesus will return to earth and set up His own kingdom; but, we won't have prepared it for Him; nor, does He expect the reinstatement of the Law.

Reconstructionism, Replacement and Kingdom Now doctrines, because of their similarities, could easily be assimilated by those working within Freemasonry to reinstate the Law and set up a worldly Utopia, following the dictates of hell-bent Masonic leaders, who surrepticiously authored a document known as *The Protocols of the Learned Wise Men of Zion*.

This document was written in such a way as to cause

the reader to believe that wealthy Jews, not Illuminist/ Freemasonry were planning to takeover the world. The *"Protocols"* have been followed to the letter by the Illuminati hierarchy to this day, blaming its contents on the Jews and attempting to usher in Fascism, like Hitler's Third Reich.

There were Christians in pre–World War II who accepted Hitler's lie that Jews were the world's problem. His socialist/democratic party took over Germany, easily fooling the unwary. By believing Hitler's occult doctrine and hellish solution, not only was the Third Reich strengthened; but, those who sided with him against God's elect are bedfellows with him in hell today.

God's chosen, whether Christian or Jew, have a place within God's kingdom. When the Jewish nation finally recognizes Jesus as their Messiah, they will rule in His Millennial Kingdom, alongside those who have given their lives to Jesus; those who have not taken the mark of the beast (Antichrist).

> *And I saw thrones, and they sat upon them, and judgment was given unto them: and I saw the souls of them that were beheaded for the witness of Jesus, and for the word of God, and which had not worshipped the beast, neither his image, neither had received his mark upon their foreheads, or in their hands; and they lived and reigned with Christ a thousand years.*

(Revelation 20:4)

God will use the Jews to reprove the world and bring

mankind to their knees. As He allows His judgments to fall, through wars, famine, death and the grave, the nation of Israel still steeped in rebellion, idolatry and witchcraft, will again suffer extreme persecution, but out of this, a remnant will be saved.

> *Esaias also crieth concerning Israel, Though the number of the children of Israel be as the sand of the sea, a remnant shall be saved.*
>
> (Romans 9:27)

> *The remnant of Israel shall not do iniquity, nor speak lies; neither shall a deceitful tongue be found in their mouth: for they shall feed and lie down, and none shall make them afraid.*
>
> (Zephaniah 3:13)

Divisive Tools

The Bible was written by Jews, to Jews, about a Jew. It was a Jew, the apostle Paul, who wrote about the church. The first Christians were Jews. They accepted the work of the cross. Even in this hour, many Jews are accepting Jesus as their Messiah. It wasn't until Peter preached to the Italian centurion that Gentiles became believers. As a nation, most Jews remain in spiritual blindness, unaware their Messiah has come. Their blindness has made a way for Gentiles to receive God's grace.

The church must not make the mistake of believing, as some do, that there is a separate covenant for the Jew, than for the believing Gentile. Each must come to the Father the same way, through faith in Jesus Christ. Dual covenant theology is a false doctrine. Sadly, one well-known televangelist has entered into this teaching, drawing multitudes into its deception.

God keeps His Word. The nation of Israel will go through severe purging of their sins during the time of Jacob's Trouble (the Tribulation); however, a tried and true remnant will accept Jesus as Messiah, and all nations will recognize God's hand upon these redeemed Jews. The same blessing of Abraham applies to both Jew and Gentile.

> *And I will make of thee a great nation, and I will bless thee, and make thy name great; and thou shalt be a blessing: And I will bless them that bless thee, and curse him that curseth thee: and in thee shall all families of the earth be blessed.*

> (Genesis 12:2-3)

Gentiles become "Jews" at heart when Jesus becomes their Savior; these are the individuals who make up the true church.

> *For he is not a Jew, which is one outwardly; neither is that circumcision, which is outward in the flesh: But he is a Jew, which is one inwardly; and circumcision is that of the heart, in the spirit, and not in the letter; whose praise is not of men, but of God.*

> (Romans 2:28-29)

The Illuminati, parents of the One World Church, have encouraged these dangerous principles and carefully laid a path of deceit to ensnare and entrap once strong denominations to believe their lies. Fritz Springmeier relates the following about the founders of the Councils of Churches:

(My)…previous large book, "Be Wise As Serpents," exposes how the Rockefellers, the Rothschilds, and J. P. Morgan, working with the Unitarians and Freemasons, created the Federal Council of Churches of Christ, the National Council of Churches, and the World Council of Churches.[45]

Illuminists work diligently to obey their god, Lucifer. Their purpose is to manipulate and control the masses. Through integration of seditious non-believers into church congregations, they subtly undermine true Biblical teaching and pit one believer against another, thereby causing strife and contention. They are well able to perform these diabolical schemes because of undetected evil spirits working with them. This is accomplished because most believers naively think no one could be that devious or hateful. However, these same evil entities use mind control and manipulation to achieve their means.

Many divisions and battles between religious elements in the world have been encouraged and supported by the Power's wealth. (The Illuminati). They have also used people under their mind control and/or blackmailed (them) to encourage religious strife. Unfortunately, many have been fooled into thinking that being devout and faithful to God is the source of religious fighting. In some areas of the world, Moslems, Christians, and others have gotten along fine for centuries. Religious tensions do spring to some degree from within the religions themselves, but the fuel to keep these fires burning and to light up conflicts often come from the Power's wealth. An obvious example is the Iran-Iraq war.[46]

Subliminal messages sent forth over the air waves are a form of psychological warfare. By these, the media has brought about change in the world's belief system, denigrating that which pertains to belief in God and Jesus Christ. Empowered by the Illuminati's wealthy influence, the media has led innocent souls to become indoctrinated with satanic ideals and, in many cases, satanic rituals.

Inasmuch as witchcraft covens are all about us, their incantations, along with misguided carnal prayers of believers, can unleash psychic power, a tool strongly used by Satan. It is vitally necessary to know how to stand against these forces and be an overcomer.

And they overcame him by the blood of the Lamb, and by the word of their testimony; and they loved not their lives unto the death.

(Revelation 12:11)

Some will knowingly deny Jesus, while others will be blinded by deception because of false and misguided teaching, and follow the "god of forces." Many will be deceived by their own "itching ears", desirous of material wealth and or fame false teachers proclaim, or the fear of man, which works a snare to their soul.

Yea, the time cometh, that whosoever killeth you will think that he doeth God service.

(John 16:2)

Paul warned of this gross apostasy. Because of

adulterated Bibles, false teaching and subliminal messages, the believer must constantly be on guard.

> *Let no man deceive you by any means: for that day shall not come, except there come a falling away first, and that man of sin be revealed, the son of perdition; who opposeth and exalteth himself above all that is called God, or that is worshipped; so that he as God sitteth in the temple of God, shewing himself that he is God.*

(2 Thessalonians 2:3-4)

Many Christian leaders have joined forces with evil "Illuminated" ones or angels of light, accepting funds from Masonic/Illuminists, or are Masons themselves, while others have totally defected from the Christian faith. One member of European royalty ...Prince Charles...is rumored to have become a Muslim, but still holds his position in the Anglican Church and embraces Catholicism, too---an ecumenist at heart.

The prince's advocacy of building mosques and temples is fascinating enough. Yet his overtures toward the world's one-billion plus Muslims have become far more extreme. According to a few Muslim sources on the internet, the prince has undergone the ceremonies necessary to "become a Muslim by the name of 'Abdus-Salem Hafidh ad-Deen,'" which means "The Guardian of faith." [47]

The One World Church includes all faiths, Masons, Muslims, Buddhists, Catholics, apostate believers, and world political leaders---all who follow, or will follow, the dictates of Lucifer. Among them are Jewish deceivers working to fulfill their plans to overtake the world and rule it. These apostate Jews are not alone, for theirs is a brotherhood that consists of Jew and Gentile alike combined of many secret societies filled with men of corrupt minds who believe gain is godliness and whose perversions have led multitudes down the path of damnation.

The Great Tribulation will soon erupt, and we need to be mindful of God's promises. We must not be a partaker of the sins of the false church. In many cases, it may mean forsaking the church of your youth or one that has compromised truth, fallen from grace or has accepted secular humanism or strange manifestations and miracles of questionable origin.

It is not anti-Semitic to point out that Jews are strong among the cryptocracies. These Jews do not believe in the true God, but worship Lucifer, as was true in Jesus' day; and were the persecutors of Jesus. Jesus rebuked the Jewish Pharisees and Saducees, recognizing their rebellion toward God.

Men and women behind these evil secret organizations rely on doublespeak and outright lies to hide their diabolical intent. They transfer guilt and accuse those who choose to expose these godless people as being the actual perpetrators of evil or of being hateful anti-Semitics. This propaganda is used to deceive and cause those who believe in the way of the cross to be criticized, ostracized and persecuted for the truth in which they believe.

The perpetrators of One World Government, its apostate One World Church, with their anti-God Luciferian philosophy are, in fact, the very ones who are anti-Semitic and determined to destroy all who believe in God, or the Lord Jesus Christ. Like the "virgin" in an earlier chapter, she wasn't a "virgin" in the true sense of the word. Nor are these criminal deceivers working for the Jews, but, are deceitful workers of iniquity.

In the wilderness, the children of Israel had not given up Egyptian occult practices. This culminated in worship of the golden calf…much like prosperity theology, another hellish doctrine. We have become a nation of weaklings. Some would sell their souls for financial gain or personal acclaim, unwilling to believe that God would permit them to suffer for His sake. Charismatic prosperity teachers have made "merchandise" of God's people, leading them into sins of presumption.

> In the Old Testament, the Israelites were drawn repeatedly to the 'ways of Egypt,' the most striking symbolical moment being the worship of the Golden Calf (Exodus 32:1-35). The Egyptian-inspired rabbinic oral teaching was later opposed by Jesus Christ, but nonetheless survived the destruction of the Second Temple in 70 A.D., after which it was gradually committed to writing by rabbis and became known as the Babylonian Talmud and the Kabbalah.

> The tyrannical discipline of the pagan priesthood of Egypt and Babylon was veiled in the Talmud beneath references to the Scriptures of the Israelites; similarly, the Kabbalah preserved an occult teaching within an occasional appearance of piety, orthodoxy,

and commentaries on the Mosaic texts of the Pentateuch."[48]

Ever so subtly, Illuminati-geared mind control is ushering multitudes into mass deception. Bombarded by altered media coverage, coupled with perverted education in schools and churches, Lucifer's agents are preparing the world to receive a dictator, one they believe will lead them to a Utopia. An ugly shadow is settling over the world, yet few seem to care, or to raise a voice against it.

CHAPTER SIX

DESTINED FOR EVIL

I will bless them that bless thee, and curse him that curseth thee: and in thee shall all families of the earth be blessed

(Genesis 12:3)

Because Abraham determined to believe God and obey His commands God made an unalterable covenant with Abraham to make of him a great nation. Isaac sired Jacob, out of whose issue were 12 sons, and Ishmael sired 12 sons of his own. These families were but a miniscule part of God's promise to Abraham.

Ishmael was the child of the flesh, not the promised child. Abraham "jumped the gun" moving presumptuously; and, as a result, his progeny have battled it out ever since. (A type and shadow of the spiritual battle believers fight each day...flesh vs spirit.) Isaac was to inherit the land mass promised to his father, while Ishmael was destined to be a wild nomad.

...call his name Ishmael; because the Lord hath heard thy affliction. And he will be a wild man; his hand will be against every man, and every man's hand against him; and he shall dwell in the presence of all his brethren.

(Genesis 16:11-12)

Isaac's sons, Jacob and Esau, struggled within Rebekah during her pregnancy. God told her she bore two nations and *"...the elder would serve the younger."* Esau foolishly gave his birthright to Jacob. He wanted instant gratification. The resultant jealousy and rivalry still exists between these two nations...Arab and Jew. *"As it is written, Jacob have I loved, but Esau have I hated."* (Romans 9:13) Esau was considered an idolater, who disobeyed the first commandment. *"Thou shalt have no other gods before Me."* (Exodus 20:3). He was guilty, as well, of despising his birthright, the rightful inheritance of the first born.

Blessed, because of wise choices, God loved Jacob. He is listed as one of the three patriarchs…Abraham, Isaac and Jacob. Out of his loins the nation of Israel was born. To this day, they are God's chosen people. Although Jacob has been falsely accused by saint and sinner alike, he was not a supplanter; but, fulfilled his God-appointed destiny when he "apparently stole" Esau's birthright under his mother's wise counsel. In the eyes of God, it was his right from birth. He couldn't steal something already his.

A Wayward Son

From Jacob's twelve sons, it is believed Dan's tribe will bring forth the Antichrist as God's instrument to judge the tribes of Israel for denial of their Messiah. If one specific thing could be said about Dan, it was this: he, too, was an idolater. That is a fact of his family's history. Scripture reveals he apparently never repented. His name is not listed among the twelve Israelite tribes sealed for protection in Revelation seven. God hates idolatry; and, Dan had "sold out," like Esau before him.

> *Ye shall make you no idols nor graven image, neither rear you up a standing image, neither shall ye set up any image of stone in your land, to bow down unto it: for I am the Lord your God.*

(Leviticus 26:1)

Dan will ultimately face an angry God! If he ever had any fear of the Lord, he would have repented of his idolatry; however, there is no evidence of that. Jacob's dying words to Dan were that his descendents would bring judgment upon the other tribes.

> *Dan shall judge his people, as one of the tribes of Israel. Dan shall be a serpent by the way, an adder in the path that biteth the horse heels, so that his rider shall fall backward. I have waited for thy salvation, O Lord.*

(Genesis 49:16-18)

As he prophesied over his sons, Jacob saw the strange and evil future of Dan. He recognized God's calling upon Dan to judge Israel; and, as if in anticipation of the tribulation and sorrows which Dan and his evil associates would bring upon his brethren, Jacob said, "I have waited for thy salvation, O Lord." This lament was like an SOS…a cry for deliverance…because of the horrendous calamities that would befall Jacob's children in generations to come.

On his deathbed, Dan acknowledged his part in the torment and attempted murder of Joseph. He admitted he had agreed with his brothers to destroy Joseph because of jealousy and anger, and that he was a liar. Dan prophesied over his own sons seeing far into the future, aware they were wayward and willful, he knew they would take the path of demonism and destruction.

> I know that in the last days ye shall depart from the Lord, and ye shall provoke Levi unto anger, and fight against Judah; but ye shall not prevail against them, for an angel of the Lord shall guide them both; for by them shall Israel stand…And whensoever ye depart from the Lord, ye shall walk in all evil and work the abominations of the Gentiles, going a-whoring after women of the lawless ones, while with all wickedness the spirits of wickedness work in you...For I have read in the book of Enoch, the righteous, that your prince is Satan….[49]

Under Egyptian bondage for four hundred years, the children of Israel became well versed in Egypt's satanic, idolatrous rites, and their adulation of almost any and everything that moved, including beetles, lice, frogs, etc. Their profane worship carried over into the wilderness experience even while Moses was in command and leading the Israelites away from Egypt.

In the wilderness, the tribes were positioned in groups of three on of the four sides of the tabernacle under the banners of four of their brothers. These standards are reminiscent of the four phases of life on planet earth, and identify with the four faces of the living creatures of Ezekiel 1:6 and 10, and Revelation 4.7; 1) a lion – an untamed animal; 2) a calf – a tame animal; 3) man – humanity; and, 4) an eagle – a fowl.

- Judah was the standard bearer under the banner of a lion. The lion is an untamed beast. Two tribes under this standard were Issachar and Zebulun. The lion is known as the king of the jungle, and rules over jungle beasts.

  Jesus Christ is the Lion from the tribe of Judah. As King of kings and Lord of lords, He reigns over untamed, unregenerate mankind, bringing them into submission under His loving care.

- Ephraim's standard was an ox. The two tribes under the standard of the ox were Manasseh and Benjamin. The ox represents a tame work animal.

  Jesus was a servant to all mankind, giving His life as a sacrifice for the salvation of mankind.

- Reuben's standard was that of a man. Simeon and Gad were also under this standard.

  Jesus was the Son of God, but the Son of man as well. He became flesh to empathize with us. He *"...was in all points tempted like as we are, yet without sin."* (Hebrews 4:15).

- Dan's standard, originally chosen by Judah, was a snake. The other two tribes under Dan's banner were Asher and Naphtali. Unwilling to have the snake as their logo, an elder in the tribe chose the eagle, representing the fowls of the air. The final choice, however, was an eagle with a serpent in his mouth. Both the serpent and the eagle are predators by nature.

Satan appeared to Adam and Eve as a serpent; or, in its alternate translation,, as a fiery red dragon. Dan's standard represented both the eagle and the serpent. As God foretold, a serpent was to *"...bite the horses' heel so that his rider fall backwards."*
(Genesis 49:17).

Dan's banner was situated on the north side of the tabernacle. Interestingly, this position to the tabernacle is a prophetic witness as to Dan's later thrust into Europe and a reflection of Lucifer's heart...his desire to be positioned *"...also upon the mount of the congregation, in the sides of the north."*
(Isaiah 14:13).

Tribe of Dan

Secret societies value the image of the eagle. It is an emblem of European royalty, as well as of the United States. This symbol is an indication of the prevalence of the tribe of Dan throughout the Roman Empire in its prime.

The eagle appears in the insignia of many nations, including ancient Rome, Nazi and modern-day Germany, Czarist Russia, and the United States…The eagle is also represented in the Great Seal of the U.S. A. and it is revered as a holy sign by Sufi Moslems.[50]

Inasmuch as Dan was considered to have traveled the course of Europe and never repented from his occult worship, it should be no surprise to discover the eagle logo throughout Europe and those whose nations comprise the former Roman Empire. Nor, should it surprise us that this bird of "prey" is esteemed by those who have made Lucifer their god. Symbolic of the sun, it is considered the embodiment of Nimrod and his many aliases. How fitting, then, that those who worship the false gods of mythology have claimed it as their symbol; but, as mentioned before, it should be remembered that it is a bird of "prey."

Herod the Great…placed an eagle (a symbol of the tribe of Dan) above the temple in the years just prior to the birth of Jesus. How significant! For the mysterious tribe of Dan appears to have laid claim to the temple, just as they may again someday, when the antichrist commits the abomination of desolation."[51]

It appears the prophecy to Dan by Jacob took root; Dan's offspring were out for revenge because of their small land grant. Through investigation, it has been discovered that the tribe of Dan is interrelated with British Royalty, the Rothschilds, and other wealthy elitists. With Gentile apostate accomplices in Masonry and the Illuminati, they have plans for the annihilation of their Israeli brothers, or any one else who continues to believe in One God.

Dan and Ephraim are not found in chapter seven of the Book of Revelation, where the twelve tribes are sealed. Both were rebellious idolaters. However, Ephraim, as was prophesied by Jacob, was to *"become a multitude of nations."* (Genesis 48:19) His destiny has undoubtedly made a great impact upon the world.

Dan's fate was to be the judge of Israel. Perverse in his thinking, he believed his brethren deliberately cheated him out of his rightful inheritance. Dan's tribe, when it was time to issue tribal land grants, was numerically the second largest tribe of all, yet, he was given only two small sections of land, barely enough to contain his large tribe. Situated in the north, his tribe leaped into Europe, settling first Sparta (ancient Greece), and then continuing to travel northwest.

It is believed his progeny scattered throughout Europe and settled as far as the British Isles. His understanding of the occult followed wherever he traveled; and his jealousy and hatred for his brethren apparently never left him.

Dan's tribe was considered the black sheep of the nation of Israel. Historians believe the tribe of Dan ruled the Greeks, the Roman Empire, and the Austro-Hungarian Empire...those rulers who used the eagle as their logo. His tribe is believed responsible for the families of the

Merovingian kings of Europe, as there are signs of his encampment throughout Europe, especially the British Isles—Wales, Scotland, Ireland, and Northern England, and among the Scan*din*avians. (The nation of Wales has as its logo a fiery red dragon. As mentioned before, this is but another definition of the serpent of Genesis 3.)

Jesus Christ was <u>not</u> the father of Mary Magdalene's children, as the Illuminati and the *Protocols of the Learned Elders of Zion,* would have us believe. Multiplied evidence proves Dan's progeny has served Satan as prophesied by Jacob and Dan himself over his sons. These Judaizers (with Masonic help) have been responsible for extreme persecution and murderous rampages against God-fearing Jews and Christians alike down through the centuries.

Some believe their lineage can be traced to the people of the British Isles. There is evidence to confirm this. Fritz Springmeier, author of *Bloodlines of the Illuminati,* has traced the numerous bloodlines of the Illuminati back to the tribe of Dan. He states:

> I have the genealogies of the British and Scottish royalty, and they go back to the Tribe of Dan. I have the genealogies of the Scottish Stuart Kings and they are intertwined with the House of Orange (which has played such a big role in modern history in the Bilderbergers Societe Generale, etc.). I have the genealogies of the LDS Mormon presidents and they go back to the Tribe of Dan. I have the genealogies of a number of American Presidents; Clinton goes back to

Scottish royalty and then back to the Tribe of Dan. About half of our Presidents go back to the same bloodline as the British Royal family.[52]

Dan's influence on early European royalty is found through their choice of long hair for power (a characteristic of the Merovees). Merovees are believed to be descendents of Samson, whose power was in his hair. Samson was another from the tribe of Dan.

> Several obscure prophecies in the Bible point to the fact that the tribe of Dan will produce the Antichrist. In the context of these prophecies, Samson's riddle may be a prophecy that the descendants of the tribe of Dan will one day try to destroy the tribe of Judah in jealous revenge for God's judgment on their idolatry. From the carcass of the young lion [Judaism] the tribe of Dan [typified by the bees] will attempt to produce a golden age [symbolized by honey]. The conspiracy of the tribe of Dan, aka the Synagogue of Satan, to steal the messianic birthright from the tribe of Judah and establish a false messianic kingdom in Israel.[53]

Names derived from the name of Dan, such as the Danube, Dardanelles, Denmark (Danmark), Scandanavia, etc., give additional proof that Dan traveled north into Europe, where he and his family established false, idolatrous practices.

The Merovingians, most of whom became European royalty, are believed to be of the tribe of Dan. J. R. Church gives evidence to show how Dan could have gone into Europe and then developed the monarchies there. His chapter in *Guardians of the Grail,* entitled, *"The Roots of the Merovingians,"* trace Dan's lineage.

> I have long believed that the tribe of Dan would somehow be involved with the rise of the antichrist…I had no concrete proof to support my theory. I could not pinpoint the whereabouts of the offspring of Dan, for the ancient tribe slipped into obscurity some 3,000 years ago. Further, there is no scripture which specifically states that the future world ruler will be from that ancient Israelite tribe. I based my theory upon the implications of a few prophetic scriptures.
>
> The prophet Daniel predicted the coming of a future usurper, indicating he could be an apostate Israelite…[54]

Church quotes Daniel: *"Neither shall he regard the God of his fathers, nor the desire of women, nor regard any god: for he shall magnify himself above all."* (Daniel 11:37). We have already seen how Dan had no regard for the God of his fathers. Church asks several interesting, provocative questions:

> If the predictions that *"Dan shall judge his people"* and *"Dan shall be a serpent"* are accurate, most of the suffering of Israel

down through the centuries has been plotted and perpetrated by the lost tribe of Dan. The question is, can we prove it? Were the leaders of imperial Rome the offspring of the tribe of Dan? Was the Syrian general, Antiochus Epiphanes, who sacrificed a pig upon the brazen altar (168 B.C.) an offshoot from the tribe of Dan? Was Alexander the Great a Danite? And what about the thrones of Europe who persecuted the Jewish people over the past 1,600 years. Do they belong to that ancient tribe?[55]

Relentless Persecution

When Jesus arrived on the scene the first time, the world's conditions were much like those in today's society: Sexual perversion was unbridled, boys and girls were sold as sex slaves. Homosexuality was practiced among "elite" bureaucrats, and idolatry flourished. Idolatry and sorcery were considered normal.

The populace elevated Herod to blasphemous reverence. In the streets, noise and clamor drowned out simple transactions for food and clothing, while vendors waxed bold in the sale of idols, including busts of government leaders.

Jesus referred to the people He walked among as an *"evil generation," "vipers"* and of their *"...father the devil."* Deep conviction moved those who heard His message of love, either to follow Him or to reject Him.

They could not deny the power of God within Him and the truth that He spoke.

Slowly, but surely, His message of love and forgiveness opened the eyes of the spiritually hungry. He gained the trust of thousands through His Word and the miracles that followed. His holy life stirred wicked temple rulers (Pharisees of Jewry) to jealousy and hatred. Unable to face the blackness of their own souls, they rejoiced when He was led to Golgotha by the Romans at their instigation, while those who loved Him wept, fearing the cause for which He stood, lost.

Intruding Wolves

Shortly after His death and resurrection, Pentecost followed. Filled with the Holy Spirit, the disciples could do no less than their Master, Jesus. They watched Him speak the truth, cast out devils, heal the sick and love the unlovely. Because of their love for Him, they eagerly shared the truth of His resurrection and the power of their new lives, no longer slaves to sin, *"...turned the world upside down...."* (Acts 17:6)

Their message astounded pagans, bewildered by the truth. When they heard it, because it cut deep with inner conviction of sin, they were often moved with choler against the very ones who brought forth the Word of God, but who prayed for their deliverance.

A small band of men and women, among them multitudes of converted Jews, were unafraid to speak the truth, even though it cost their reputations, homes, families and lives. With eternity's values in view, and while the blood flowed in the streets, the church grew strong and gained a tremendous following of new converts; those stirred by the visual peace and sincerity of the testimonies of suffering believers.

Satan was not content to stop when the blood flowed. He had bigger plans, which he thought would grant him the position above God he so desired. True to his character of pride and arrogance, he pressed on to undermine the church, by infiltrating their ranks with his followers, subtly bringing dissension and division among the believers and new converts. His tactics remain the same today, and has caused many to lose their first love for Jesus, because they are unaware of Satan's treacherous, diabolical ways.

During the time of the church of Ephesus, between 70 A.D. and 170 A.D., many within the church did leave their first love. The word *Ephesus* means to *"let go"*. They let go and enjoined the doctrine of the Nicolaitanes. Jesus' message to Ephesus was: *"But this thou hast, that thou hatest the deeds of the Nicolaitanes, which I also hate."* (Revelation 2:6). The meaning of the word *Nicolaitane* is explicit. According to Clarence Larkin:

> They were not a sect, but a party in the Church who were trying to establish a "Priestly Order." Probably trying to model the Church after the Old Testament order of Priests, Levites, and common people. This is seen in the meaning of the word, which is from "Niko" to conquer, to overthrow, and "Laos," the people or laity.

The object was to establish a "Holy Order of Men", and place them over the laity, which was foreign to the New Testament plan, and call them not pastors, but Clergy, Bishops, Archbishops, Cardinals, Popes. Here we have the origin of the degree of "Apostolic Succession," and the separation of the Clergy from the Laity, a thing that God "hates."[56]

As in the world, where men are admired so as to become considered "gods," men in church positions copied the world around them and were elevated into places of reverence and admiration. Paul alerted the church that wolves would creep in among the flock after he departed. *"For I know this, that after my departing shall grievous wolves enter in among you, not sparing the flock."* (Acts 20:29)

The church began deteriorating, but not without warning. Jesus warned of deceivers, and the apostles cautioned the devout in each of the epistles from Romans through Jude. Deceivers moved among the people ever so slyly, infiltrating their once pure minds with subtle lies. Ardor and fire cooled, letting chill winds of paganism break through the walls of faith, baring cracks in the foundation and holes in the walls, corroding the teachings of the Lord and apostles.

From 170 A.D. to 313 A.D., Roman emperors from Nero to Diocletian unmercifully persecuted believers. They were fed to lions and hung on crosses. Once fearful Peter, sound in the faith, was hung upside down, no longer fearful, but courageous. There seemed to be no let-up in newly devised torture by their persecutors.

After Jesus' death, the church had become a major power with which to contend, and was one of the main reasons persecution took place with such vengeance. Emperors, who were worshipped as gods, did not like competition, nor would they stand for any interference in their perverted lifestyles, which the masses fearfully failed to confront. In many cases, average citizens were indulging in the same sins as their leaders and turned their heads the other way.

Enter Constantine

Constantine was acclaimed a "Christian," but he was pagan to the core. He saw the advantages politically of "marrying" the church to the state. It was the same pattern Nimrod used in his kingdom; although, Constantine most likely was unaware of how closely he followed Nimrod's evil example.

From the period of Nero through Diocletian, the blood baths against Christians and any other citizen who did not agree with their heinous crimes continued relentlessly. Constantine saw a way of uniting both political and religious factions by bringing the pagans and cold, Ephesus-type church members under his domination.

During the persecution of the Jews during Pharaoh's time, *"...the more they afflicted them, the more they multiplied and grew."* (Exodus 1:12). So it was during the time of the Smyrna church. Believers in Smyrna planted their "seed faith" with their lives. The earth was filled with the bodies of those who believed in the resurrection of the dead. In spite of the massive pogroms, the gospel grew strong and became a dominating power that could not be dismissed. The scent of myrrh in their dying testimonies moved others to know beyond a shadow of a doubt that there was life after death, and many new believers willingly followed the martyrs, knowing that allegiance to Jesus would seal their own fate.

Constantine seized the opportunity to expand his earthly kingdom. That opportunity came through a set of circumstances, one written in the heavens, which was to influence not only his life, but the future degradation of the church. His influence ushered pagan idol worship into the church, and apostasy fell in line. The new church/state became known as Catholicism. John's vision in Revelation 17 reveals the depths of that apostasy.

> When Emperor Constantine supposedly became a Christian in A. D. 313 (really a clever political maneuver), he gave freedom to Christians as well as official status alongside paganism to the Christian church. Since the church was not a recognized religious body in the empire, Constantine, as emperor, had to be acknowledged as its de facto head... Interested not in the truth of the gospel but in unifying the empire, Constantine was the first ecumenist and introduced that error into the persecution-wearied church.[57]

Under the Roman Emperor Diocletian's rule:

> All Bibles had to be surrendered to the authorities, all churches were to be destroyed, all Christian worship was forbidden, all clergy were to be imprisoned, and all citizens of the empire were to sacrifice to the pagan gods on pain of death.[58]

What a contrast between Constantine and Diocletian. Churches were destroyed by Diocletian, but Constantine built them and incorporated pagan rites into their worship. The term "Bishop" was used among the Nicolaitanes within the church at Ephesus. Constantine rose to the occasion and apostate, deceived Christians proclaimed him "Bishop of Bishops."

While some are fearful of the invasion of Islam, we need to be more concerned about a form of godliness that will be called "Christian" and will worship a "Christ," but not Jesus Christ. For the Roman Empire, in its revised two-legged stance, as prophesied and envisioned by the Prophet Daniel will consist of a church/state religion, the final *harlot* church on planet earth and known as, Babylon, Mother of Harlots, or the New Age Movement. All "bloodless", Jesus-denying religions will flow into her. Her roots began in Babylon, then spread out into Rome and at present are being reestablished through the European Common Market...the Revived Roman Empire under the Antichrist's rule.

CHAPTER SEVEN

DOCTRINES OF DEVILS

Now the Spirit speaketh expressly, that in the latter times some shall depart from the faith, giving heed to seducing spirits, and doctrines of devils....

(1Timothy 4:1)

Lucifer's demonic hosts and self-serving followers have sold out to him in agreement with his sinister plots to overthrow the throne of God. His "ministers" often are called angels of light, as was he. They appear to look good, but they are inherently evil. Secret societies and religious cults have the same characteristics. They may seem completely harmless, but they are deadly. To all outward signs their works may be beneficial to society, but theirs is a hidden agenda. Demon-inspired lies are cleverly manipulated to trap the naive. Once caught in their web of deceit, few escape.

The Illuminati backs many religious bodies, among them Roman Catholicism, Mormonism, Jehovah's Witnesses, Unity and various other cults. Unwilling to accept the simplicity of the gospel, many are drawn into their false teaching and doctrines of devils.

The seeds of any cult sprout straight from hell. Mormonism, because of Joseph Smith, is somewhat of a plagiarism of Masonry. Freemasonry *is* considered a religion out of which Mormonism developed. Jehovah's Witnesses claim the 144,000 to be their chosen "witnesses," whereas the 144,000 of Revelation are God's chosen

Jewish remnant, sealed before the outpouring of the seven years' tribulation…Jacob's Trouble.

The above cults evolved out of societies of men who worshipped Lucifer and denied Jesus Christ as Lord, or, are often being adulated as a "god" themselves, as, for example, Roman Catholic popes. In addition, seducers have, as previously mentioned, cleverly promoted a lie claiming that Jesus Christ and Mary Magdalene were lovers. This strategic maneuver was planned to psychologically prepare the masses to discredit Jesus and be ready to accept the man of sin, Satan's son of perdition.

Jessie Penn-Lewis in *War on the Saints,* warned the danger of following such false doctrines. She mentioned the following characterizations of more sinister cults, each of which denies sin, the need of a savior and the work of the cross. "Christian Science; Theosophy; Spiritism; New Theology."[59]

According to Penn-Lewis, (these) are within the "Christianized World." She continues:

> In the heathen world: Mahommadism (Islam); Confucianism; Buddism, etc., No Saviour, no cross, a "moral" religion, with man his own Saviour.

> Idolatry as the worship of demons…No knowledge of a Saviour, or of his Calvary sacrifice, but true knowledge of the evil powers, which they endeavour to propitiate, because they have proved them to be existent.[60]

These, and other Jesus-denying religions, are being courted by Catholicism to bring them all under her cloak… the cloak of the "Mother Church." Since the principles found in false religions stem from the same sources, Ancient Wisdom and idol worship, their acceptance of Catholicism will not be a difficult transition, especially when they come to believe the Catholic Church accepts any and all beliefs and tolerates sin.

Catholicism depicts Jesus as still hanging on the cross, whereas He arose victorious over the grave. Salvation for mankind means an empty cross and an empty tomb. He's alive. He is risen! Death has lost its sting.

Aside from Catholicism, the best known and most influential "religion," is one that is not considered a religion at all, but in reality is. Even though Catholicism has had its followers en masse the world over, this religion is ruthlessly manipulated by another far more deadly one---Freemasonry. Together, they are working with cryptocracies the world over in an effort to unite church and state under one leader, the Antichrist.

A Beast

Albert Pike's statue stands tall in Washington, D. C., however, dubious this commemoration, he is revered by Masons most everywhere as the author of their "bible", *Morals and Dogma.* Pike was not a man of excellent citizenry and upright morality as the statue would have you believe. In fact, quite the opposite is true. Pike was a convicted felon for the act of treason.

> …Albert Pike, a 33° Mason, has a place
> of honor within our nation's capitol in

Washington, D.C. This former Sovereign Grand Commander, whose commentary on Freemasonry's rituals, *Morals and Dogma*, is a textbook for all Masons, issued instructions on July 14, 1889, to the Supreme Councils of the World identifying the Master whom Masons universally worship and venerate.[61]

He deserved recognition all right, that of an antichrist pervert, one which could be considered a "beast", as he was, as his writings confirm, a worshipper of Lucifer. His writing of the *Morals and Dogma* placed him in a highly elevated position within Freemasonry.

John Daniel, author and researcher, in his, *Scarlet and the Beast,* asserts that during the Civil War, Pike obtained the assistance of Indians to have Union soldiers scalped. Others have attested that they were still alive during this massacre.. Pike was later pardoned for this treasonous act by President Andrew Johnson. Johnson caved in to the pressure exerted by the Masons to acquit Pike. For Pike's pardon, Johnson was given the doubtable honor and distinction of becoming a 32° Mason in only one day.

As noted by Mr. Daniel, one of Pike's notorious fetes was the founding of the Ku Klux clan, which basically was a name change from the Knights of the Golden Circle, a Masonic Order to which 33° Jesse James belonged. Pike, who had been a Confederate General, ordered James to rob northern banks to gain monies to renew the Civil War.

As to his moral character, Pike was known to deliver kegs of liquor and wagon loads of "scarlet women" into the backwoods of the southern states for orgies. In physical appearance, he was morbidly obese.

As Supreme Grand Commander of Freemasonry in July of 1889, he issued the following statement to the 23 Supreme Councils of the world:

> That which we must say to the crowd is— we worship a God, but it is the God that one adores without superstition...To you, Sovereign Grand Inspector Generals, we say this: that you may repeat it to the brothers of the 32nd, 31st, and 30th degrees---The Masonic religion should be, by all of us initiates of the high degrees, maintained in the purity of the Luciferian doctrine.[62]

Thus, it is evident that there is an evil "core" within Masonry, one whose outward philanthropies appear beneficial to all mankind, and which, by their seeming philanthrophic goodness, draw unsuspecting individuals into their brotherhood. The other side of that coin is a carefully concealed, treacherously evil organization, bent on destruction of families, governments, Christianity and anything, or anyone, standing in their way.

John Daniel, in his book, *Scarlet and the Beast,* gives evidence of the wicked lies behind Shriners, a well-known philanthropic "cover" within the Masons. Most think highly of these men, not realizing they are servants of Allah...not Almighty God.

> They are jokingly referred to as 32 1/2° Masons, since only 32° Scottish Rite Masons and 13° York Rite Masons could join the Shrine...that changed after the 9/11 attacks on America in 2001 by Moslem terrorists. For you see, Shriners take an oath to 'Allah,

the god of Arab, Moslem and Mohammedan,
the god of our fathers.'"[63]

Many of these Masons and their companions in deceit are extremely wealthy elitists, CEOs, politicians, heads of state, lawyers, bankers…apostate Jews, crypto-Jews, or pseudo-Jews and/or Gentiles, intent on building a superior race, no matter whom they destroy by their false standards. Scripture clearly delineates this class of evil men, warning that their riches will fail them in the end.

Fraternal Penalties

Freemasonry's oaths require strict obedience on the threat of death. Their manuals state a Mason can be severely punished if Masonic secrets are divulged, and they give directions for the execution of violators. These executions are to be performed by fellow fraternal members. History records heinous crimes of torture and murder carried out by fellow lodge brothers whenever a brother has, of his own free will, violated those vows.

> A heavy burden is placed on the shoulders of a Mason when he joins the lodge. He is no longer his own man. He must obey unseen powers set above him, whether he agrees with them or not, or else he pays the penalty…[64]

John Daniel wrote the introduction to Charles Finney's book on Freemasonry. In this introduction, he explained that William Morgan, a Royal Arch Mason of thirty years, converted to Christianity and became aware of the Mason's sinister intrusion into the development of our country. Morgan was made an example to the brotherhood and was murdered for divulging the secrets and oaths within the Order.

These oaths are critical, because behind them lies the reason for the murder of William Morgan and the subsequent cover-up of the crime. First, a Blue Lodge Mason (degrees 1-3) agrees to ever conceal and never reveal any of the secret arts, parts or points of the hidden mysteries of Ancient Freemasonry. Second he promises to always be ready to obey all Masonic authority set above him, and never cheat, wrong, nor defraud a fellow Mason. Then he takes the following blood oath:

> 'All this I most solemnly and sincerely promise and swear, with a firm and steadfast resolution, to keep and perform the same without any equivocation, mental reservation or secret evasion of mind whatever, binding myself under a no less penalty than that of having my throat cut across, my tongue torn out by its roots and buried in the rough sands of the sea at low water mark, where the tide ebbs and flows twice in twenty-four hours...having my breast torn open, my heart plucked out and given as a prey to the beasts of the field and the fowls of the air… having my body severed in twain, my bowels taken from thence and burned to ashes, and the ashes scattered to the four winds of heaven, that no

trace or remembrance may be had
of so vile and perjured a wretch as I,
should I ever knowingly violate this
my solemn obligation of an Entered
Apprentice Mason...Fellow Craft
Mason...Master Mason. So help me,
God, and keep me steadfast in the due
performance of the same.'[65]

To some this may sound like pure fantasy. The
truth is, death threats have been carried out over the years,
and often sentences reversed in cases of serious crimes,
all because the judge and/or the jury were Freemasons.
(Reader: Do you now understand why our court system
is so liberal? Masons hold high positions within the
governments of the world.)

What appears to be a nice, comfortable organization
will deliberately evade truth and justice if it suits their
purposes of devilment and deceit. Members have controlled
governments and started revolutions following the dictates
of those within the higher degrees of the Fraternity. By
sheer numbers and financial strength, their influence has
shaped the destiny of nations, including that of the United
States.

For instance, it was the Masonic-ordered death of
Archduke Ferdinand of Austria-Hungary that set off World
War I.

Consider the military trial of the Freemason,
Cabrinovic, assassin of the Archduke
Ferdinand of Austria, Hungary, a fateful
event that touched off the deadly and fiery
conflict of World War I...Asked if he had

conspired with other Freemasons to murder the Archduke and thus set off a saga of anarchy and mayhem throughout Europe, Cabrinovic told the military court, "Yes, I knew we were all Freemasons, and this strengthened my resolve…Freemasonry strengthened my intention. In Freemasonry it is permitted to kill.[66]

Knowing the leniency and sometimes criminal intent of our own court system, we should undoubtedly consider the fact that Masons protect each other and, will lie on witness stands, even in cases where thievery, murder, or treason have been committed, if a brother is involved, or the brotherhood approves a cover up.

Can the reader begin to understand the extent that our own court system is now controlled by Freemason/Illuminists…men, who are lawless and intent upon government takeover…treating the masses like so much cattle on their way to the slaughter house?

When we examine the historical record of the world's most despicable mass murderers and revolutionaries, we find that almost all of them were members of Freemasonry and other secret societies of the Illuminati:

Robespierre was a Freemason; Weishaupt was a Freemason; Napoleon was a Freemason; Lenin was a Freemason; Stalin was a Freemason; Mussolini was a Freemason, Truman and Roosevelt were Freemasons; Ariel Sharon is a Freemason; Bill Clinton is a Freemason; Fidel Castro is a Freemason.[67]

Tomes could be written about Freemasonry and its influence on men and women throughout the world. Although considered a "fraternal organization," it is a powerful worldwide religion whose auxiliary, the Eastern Star, works hand-in-hand with the group. Those who become members usually join for social or financial benefits accorded to members in good standing.

Contrary to what is portrayed to the public, or to unsuspecting initiates, this is not a philanthropic organization. That is pretentious at the very least, for there is within its membership a secret clandestine group that adheres to Egyptology and the false gods Isis, Osiris and Horus.

David Bay of Cutting Edge Ministries has thoroughly researched Masonry, false teachings and the last-days' apostasy that is invading the Church and political scene. Bay quotes extensively in one of his articles on Masonry from Frederick de Clifford's book *Egypt, Cradle of Ancient Masonry*. In his article, Mr. Bay states:

> Before we go any further, I believe it might be helpful to define the term, Paganism, as the Bible defines it. Many people have a very vague concept of what this term means, and that kind of understanding simply will not suffice if we are to communicate to you exactly what kind of religion Freemasonry truly is. The Biblical definition of Paganism is succinctly stated in Romans 1:25, "Who changed the truth of God into a lie, and worshipped and served the creature more than the Creator, who is blessed for ever. Amen."[68]

Lies, Lies and More Lies

Ancient Mysteries, with its perverse sexual practices, have been revitalized. Cultists are "believers," all right, but in gods and goddesses and the possibility of becoming "gods," as Satan promised Eve. The same old lie has been repeated in every cult, every false doctrine and every strategy known to "hoodwink" the credulous into "the lie," which will ultimately lead them to a devil's hell. David Bay continues:

> The greatest single drive of mankind is sex. When you add this fact to the Biblical definition of Paganism, then we should not be too surprised to discover that Pagans are very preoccupied with sex in the practice of their religion, and express this preoccupation with sexual symbols. In Paganism, the entire world is thought to be dependent upon "balance" between the Male and the Female Principles. This belief is usually expressed in symbols with a Male Phallic symbol and a Female symbol. Of course, the Male Phallic symbol must be long and narrow and the Female symbol must be open and expansive.

> In the section from de Clifford's book, we were shocked to see that he graphically presented one of the oldest Pagan sexual symbols known. In this the pertinent section, the Male Phallic symbol is the river, especially the River Nile; the Female symbol is the Earth surrounding the Nile. In this sexual symbolism, Osiris is

the name of the Male River phallic symbol, and Isis is the name of the Female symbol, the rich black earth of land surrounding the Nile. The "activity" spoken of by the River, Osiris, is sexual relations with the Earth, Isis.[69]

The Washington Monument dedicated to George Washington, who was a Mason, is a long, thin structure with thirteen tiers forming the top pyramid. It is an obelisk, dedicated to the "god" Horus. This structure symbolizes an erect male phallus, a Masonic sign, and part of Egyptian worship. This is not the only sign in this "Christian" nation that has had its influence from Masonry. It would shock many to know the very layout of Washington, D.C., is based on Masonic symbolism, including a pentagram, the five-pointed star also known as Baphomet, which some say is the seal of Satan.

Hoodwinked

Remember William Morgan, who faithfully followed the Masonic oaths all the way to the top, had become a 33rd degree Mason, and was subsequently murdered by his "fellows"? Three of these fellow Masons carried out their oaths to the brotherhood.

> When a brother reveals any of our great secrets; whenever, for instance, he tells anything about Boaz, or Tubalcain, or Jachin, or that awful Mahhah-bone, or even whenever a minister prays in the name of Christ in any of our assemblies, you must always hold yourself in readiness, if called upon, to cut his throat from ear to ear, pull out his tongue by the roots, and bury his body at the bottom of some lake or pond.[70]

Morgan was "hoodwinked." A hood was placed over his head, secured by a rope, and he was left for several hours in that state. Then he was pulled by the rope and pushed to his death into the Niagara River. This act was confirmed by deathbed confessions of Masonic perpetrators who performed the crime to fulfill their Masonic oaths. Morgan was not, nor has he been, the only one to go to an early grave because of the divulgence of Masonic rites.

After his disappearance and later discovered remains, there was severe unrest and extremely angry reaction among the American people, making it necessary for Masonry to take a lower "key"; at that time, Freemasonry became a "hush-hush" organization. They apparently disappeared from the world scene only to revive later in greater numbers. Today, this cryptocracy circles the globe, and is in most every major government.

What was the mystery that surrounded Morgan's death and the secrecy that suddenly hid the Illuminati and led Masons deeper behind closeted, clandestine meetings? Upon Morgan's disclosure, the Masons followed Adam Weishaupt's instructions. Weishaupt was a former Mason, whose development of the Illuminati was to "purify" the Masonic ideology. Weishaupt was a Rothschild "puppet".

With Weishaupt's instructions in mind, it is understandable why there are so many covert organizations. Many operate as business organizations, yet conduct clandestine meetings working for a New World Order.

Masquerade

Over the centuries, many innocent Jews and

"willfully ignorant," or apostate Christians, have been sucked into Masonry under false pretenses. They are made to believe that this is a Christian organization, when it is a clever masquerade to seduce souls into satanic doctrine.

Recently, the History Channel released a program about secret societies and the Masons. To that channel's credit, they gave a fairly balanced report, showing the cover-up within these groups and recognizing that conspiracy theorists might be right after all.

Within the same week, the Discovery Channel had a program about the Masons. They openly showed the first three levels of Masonic rites, which do not disclose the truth of the Order. This was a psychological ploy to make the Order appear as an innocent organization, filled with nothing but "good ole' boys", who are really harmless and intent on doing good works. The majority of Masons are, for the most part, a well-manipulated, blindly led, group, which serves as a front organization for the Illuminati's One World Order Antichrist scheme.

Desirous of financial gain, leaders of these covert organizations have sold arms, supplies and military secrets to both sides in a war. They manipulate the stock market to their advantage, doing whatever it takes to bring money into their pockets and men into submission.

Once in the "fold," the deceived submit by sharing some of their own secrets. This has caused countless men to forgo leaving the organizations for fear of their personal secret lives being exposed. In some cases, as in Skull and Bones, Masons and Illuminati, they are informed of their permanent removal (murder) should they disclose the secrets and/or oaths of their respective societies.

Those who believe in one God are hated by these organizations, which tout Communism and Fascism. These henchmen/women of Satan want nothing to do with any God, save theirs. Therefore, to see their plans for world take over carried out, they plan to make "cannon fodder" of any who refuse to go along with their satanic implemented creeds.

The booklet, *Protocols of the Wise Men of Zion,* has been quite effective, causing many innocents, both Christian and Jew, to be put to death for the very crimes of which these occult groups were guilty. Through the Illuminati, the plans within this booklet have been carried out to the letter. Why should we be surprised if they present their leader to the world, and he becomes accepted by the masses…the demonic Antichrist?

CHAPTER EIGHT

EVIL CONSPIRATORS

*But evil men and seducers shall wax worse
and worse, deceiving and being deceived.*
(2 Timothy 3:13)

Out of the paganism of the Church of Rome emerged
the Jesuit priesthood. Jewish-born Adam Weishaupt
became a Catholic Jesuit priest. At one time, Weishaupt was
Professor of Canon Law at the University of Ingolstadt in
Bavaria. He left the priesthood to develop an organization,
which would become known as "The Illuminati."

According to Salem Kirban:

> Weishaupt, although born a Jew, was a
> convert to Roman Catholicism. He became
> a Jesuit priest only to break with that order to
> form his own secret organization. One of the
> reasons for secrecy was to avoid attacks by
> the Bavarian Jesuits.[71]

It is important to recognize the weight of the
Catholic Church upon Weishaupt. Through it, he had
accepted many false concepts, especially those acquired
during his participation as a Jesuit priest. As we have
learned, Constantine's influence had incorporated many
pagan doctrines into the entire structure of Catholicism.
That aside, however, it was Mayer Amschel Rothschild

who directed Weishaupt and backed him financially to establish the Illuminati.

> 1770: Mayer Amschel Rothschild draws up plans for the creation of the "Illuminati," and entrusts…Adam Weishaupt, a Crypto-Jew (a Jew who pretends he's not Jewish) who is outwardly Roman Catholic, with its organization and development. The "Illuminati" is to be based upon the teachings of the Talmud, which is, in turn, the teachings of Rabbinical Jews. It is to be called the "Illuminati," which is a Luciferian term which means "keepers of the light."[72]

May 1st of 1776, May Day, known as a signal of distress, should have alerted the world that mischief was afoot. May Day is observed by cultists everywhere. On that day, Weishaupt completed the Illuminati's organization. It may have been his aim from its onset to finish on that particular occult-celebrated holiday, known as Beltane.[73]

> …The purpose of the "Illuminati" is to divide the non-Jews through political, economic, social, and religious means. The plan is for the opposing sides of the goyim (non-Jews) to be armed whilst incidents are to be provided in order for them to fight amongst themselves; destroy national governments; destroy religious institutions; and eventually destroy each other.[74]

Rothschild, in close association with Lucifer, laid out the plans, and bid Weishaupt to carry them out.

Weishaupt...infiltrates the Continental Order of Freemasons with this "Illuminati" doctrine and establishes lodges of the Grand Orient to be their secret headquarters. This all under the orders and finance of Mayer Amschel Rothschild, and the concept subsequently spreads into Masonic Lodges worldwide to the present day.

Weishaupt also recruits 2,000 paid followers including the most intelligent men in the field of arts and letters, education, science, finance, and industry. They are instructed on the following methods in order to control people.

1) Use monetary and sex bribcry to obtain control of men already in high places...

2) Use...faculties of colleges and universities...to cultivate students possessing exceptional mental ability as well as belonging to well-bred families with

international leanings…(give them) …special training in internationalism, or rather the notion that only a one-world government can put an end to recurring war and strife. Such training is to be provided by scholarships to those selected by the "Illuminati."

3) The above men/women influenced and trapped into the "Illuminati"…are to be used as agents and placed behind the scenes of all governments as experts and specialists…bring about the destruction of the governments and religions they are elected or appointed to serve….

4) …obtain absolute control of the press…so that all news and information could be slanted in order to make the masses believe that a one-world government is the *only* solution to the world's many and varied problems.[75]

Future Designs

The pyramid and triangle are significant symbols within Masonic worship. The All-Seeing Eye was idolized in Egypt, identified as "the eye of Osiris," a god of Ancient Mysteries. The All-Seeing Eye is a part of Freemasonry's imagery; and does not represent the Supreme Being of Christians, but, a god of mythology, otherwise identified as Nimrod. In mythology, Horus, Osiris' son, plucked out his eye and gave it to Osiris.

This symbol of the pyramid and All-Seeing Eye is visible on the back of our United States' one-dollar bill, and reveals Illuminati influential power within our government, or the shadow government, controlled by money barons of the world. However, it was Weishaupt who first incorporated the pyramid with the "eye" above it into the Illuminati; and later approved for our national seal by Franklin Delano Roosevelt.

> When Weishaupt designed the sun-rayed "mountain of god" as a capstone hovering above an unfinished pyramid, he placed with the triangle an eye like the eye of man—known to Masons as the "Eye of Providence," or the "All-Seeing Eye." According to Freemasonry, the All-Seeing Eye is "an important symbol of the Supreme Being". It is a rendition of the "Egyptian eye of Osiris."[76]

Weishaupt's Order of the Illuminati copied the Masons in their use of secret rituals:

Every member spied on every other member. Each month the Novice had to deliver to Weishaupt a sealed letter which revealed every aspect of his relationship with his superior.[77]

There were three levels or classes within the organization over which one member was considered the head (or superior). Weishaupt bragged:

> The most admirable thing of it all is that great Protestant and reformed theologians (Lutherans and Calvinists) who belong to our Order really believe they see in it the true and genuine mind of the Christian religion. Oh man, what can not you be brought to believe?[78]

Weishaupt was a "slick," devious, con artist. His charm could make men of influence and means believe they were unworthy of higher ranks. "They must be made to believe that the low degree that they have reached is the highest."[79]

The three levels that could be obtained in Weishaupt's Illuminati were:

1) Novice; 2) Minerval; 3) Illuminated Minerval.

When a Novice advanced to Minerval, a clandestine ceremony revealed those who had also been promoted to the Minerval grade. A newly initiated Minerval was permitted to know secret signs and given a password, but was still not allowed to know who was in the Illuminated

Minerval.

When a member had reached the grade of Illuminated Minerval, he learned the ultimate aims of the Order:

1. Abolition of all ordered government
2. Abolition of private property
3. Abolition of inheritance
4. Abolition of patriotism
5. Abolition of all religion
6. Abolition of the family (via the abolition of marriage)
7. Creation of a world government[80]

The citizenry has become desensitized. The Illuminati doctrine is so much a part of society, few recognize its danger; and, because of tainted news media, they are constantly lulled into sleep. The stealth by which these plans easily invaded our American way of life can only be attributed to our ignorance and naivety.

Infiltration

Whcn Weishaupt was able to infiltrate the Masons, it happened in great part to the work of Baron Adolph Knigge. Together, Weishaupt's cunning, Knigge's connections and Rothschild's money, advanced these far-reaching, diabolical plans, and by 1782, their alliance became a reality.

On July 16, 1782 at the Congress of Wilhelmsbad, an alliance between Illuminism and Freemasonry was finally sealed. On that day the leading secret societies were infiltrated, and to some degree, united...more than 3 million members![81]

Baron Adolph Knigge was one of the most prominent and powerful "...members of those who then became Masonic Illuminati."[82] Initiates took pseudonyms. Weishaupt was called, "Spartacus"; Herr von Zwack, his assistant, became "Cato", and Knigge, was called, "Philo". Knigge was used to bring the original Order of the Illuminati "...along Masonic lines".[83]

Weishaupt feared the Bavarians, and for good reason. Through an "accident" the evil plans were discovered; and, "...a voluminous array of documents were found in Illuminati headquarters."[84] It was on March 2, 1785, "...when the Bavarian government banned both the Illuminati and the Freemasons."[85]

The Bavarian government heard four leading members of the Illuminati testify before a Court of Inquiry exposing the Satanic nature of its aims. A voluminous array of documents was found in Illuminati headquarters. The Bavarian government published them to warn all the other countries of Europe.[86]

The Bavarian government had done all in its power to expose the ruthless Illuminati Order in Europe. It was apparently too late.

By the time this Bavarian Illuminati Order

had been exposed, Illuminism had already spread into more than a dozen countries… Those leaders who had not already fallen under Illuminati influence found its plans so extraordinary that they refused to take it seriously.[87]

Many members were tried and convicted by the Bavarian government; however, they, along with Weishaupt, were able to flee Bavaria, probably through the secret channels of the brotherhood. By then, the Order had gained strength in the 13 new Colonies, and infiltrated the United States before the Constitution was in place. Among one of the strong Illuminati lodges within the new Colonies was the one in New York City. Its members included Governor DeWitt Clinton, Clinton Roosevelt, and Horace Greeley. A Lodge in Virginia was identified with Thomas Jefferson.[88]

It was Clinton Roosevelt who made quite clear the aim and intent of the Illuminati and its companion brotherhood, Freemasonry. In a book which he wrote, *Science of Government,* he said:

> …there is no God of justice to order
> things aright on earth: if there be a
> God, he is a malicious and revengeful
> being, who created us for misery.[89]

With statements like this, and men like this in

control, it is easy to see the depravity of the men who formed these secret societies, and the adherents who have followed them. The relationship to the Roosevelt's and Clinton's is also undeniable. Political families have been interwoven throughout the history of the United States.

In 1834, Giuseppe Mazzini became the head of the Illuminati and held that position until 1872. He undoubtedly promoted the occult within the organization, for it was Mazzini who led in the creation of the "…Theosophical Society, and the I. W. A. (1st Communist International)."[90] He believed in a "…unified Germany under a Masonic-led Prussian."[91]

During the time Mazzini was Director,

> …an obscure intellectual joined one of the branch organizations of the Illuminati called the League of the Just. His name was Karl Heinrich Marx. Karl Marx denounced his Jewish birth and the Christianity of his parents, who were converts.[92]

These three evil, apostate conspirators have shaped the affairs of nations and directly or indirectly caused the deaths of multitudes of innocents. Once an individual turns apostate, they fall easy prey to Satan. Blinded by his influence and seduced into his fold, Satan is gleeful about their betrayal of Christ, for it enlarges his camp and brings the reproach against Jesus, he so desires.

The Bible informs us that apostasy will continue gaining strength until the Antichrist steps on the scene with his henchmen, steeped in anti-God Communist ideology, as developed by men like Marx,[93] Mazzini and Weishaupt. Incidentally,

> May 1st, the day the Illuminati was founded, has become known as May Day, the universal holiday of communist countries. Weishaupt's Illuminati Colors were 'red' to represent the human blood to be shed in all future revolutions. Every May Day the former Soviet Union flaunted its military might under thousands of red banners, as the Red Army marched down Red Square behind awesome weapons of war created to spill man's blood into rivers of red.[94]

Then, there was Frances "Fanny" Wright, whose promotion of an Illuminati Auxiliary encouraged the Communist ideology. The development of the "feminist" viewpoint that has caused women to become more independent, taking on masculine positions to their own detriment, was likely spawned by women such as Ms.Wright.

> An English woman, Frances "Fanny" Wright, came to New York in 1829 to give a series of lectures promoting the Women's Auxiliary... She advocated Communism. She also spoke of equal opportunity and equal rights, atheism, free love and the emancipation of women. Clinton Roosevelt (an ancestor of FDR), Charles Dana and Horace Greeley were appointed to raise funds for this new

undetaking.[95]

The connection between Catholicism, Freemasonry, Communism, Fascism and the Illuminati is clear. To those who believe these creeds dead or defeated, watch carefully as history repeats itself. Remember, they gain adherents to their diabolical plans by subterfuge. It starts with socialistic intrusion such as social security, socialized medicine, or other so-called benefits to the populace, until an unwary public believes they can't get along without them. The common thread is the thrust for the building of a One World Government under a tyrannical ruler of their choosing. This ruler is waiting off stage, ready to make his appearance, in a socialist/democracy, much like Hitler's Third Reich.

> Once Weishaupt's organization was established, the Illuminati began to use any means available to facilitate its destruction of Christianity and civilization. Its members were involved in devil worship and they actively worked to uphold Satan's initiatives. The Order solidified its control over the Masonic lodges of Europe, and became the leaders of the one-world movement.[96]

This statement should make any man, woman, or child, wary of any organization, government official, or presidency, that advocates a New World Order. Their single-minded desire is to abolish the rights and freedoms that we, in the United States of America, have taken for granted far too long and have slowly watched slip away. These rights not only apply to our national liberty, but freedom to worship as Christians. The church in the U. S. will soon come under government dictatorship; and, those who hold a non-profit status will be forced to obey the dictates of the government, or lose their church and perhaps their lives.

Within this web of secrecy are many, varied, concealed societies. Secrecy is a valuable tool for all of their diabolical schemes. As Weishaupt said of the unwary members:

> These people swell our numbers and
> fill our treasury; get busy and make
> these people nibble at our bait...but
> do not tell them our secrets. They
> must be made to believe that the low
> degree that they have reached is the
> highest.[97]

Weishaupt utilized Freemasons to weld the Illuminati together. The plot was to deceive and delude the masses for monetary gain. Yes, it is all about money and power! It was simple; play on their pride, and that way they would not question the possibility of deception.

Inseparable Institutions

The Illuminati and the Freemason standards are inseparable. They are working toward the same end. David Smith describes the Illuminati's plans, which have been carried out almost to the letter to this very day:

> The only way to trace their movements is to find groups or organizations working toward the same goal as the Illuminati... the DESTRUCTION of NATIONAL SOVEREIGNTY and the establishment of a One World Government, a "Novus Ordo Seclorum."[98]

Of course, such visionary plans for subversive activity would be rejected and disputed by ordinary citizens...those who have fought for the right to be free from dictatorships within their respective countries. It has seldom been the majority that rules; but, by force and intimidation, small subversive groups have edged out the majority rule. This has always been the case to install the satanic plans of the Luciferians.

What a different world this would be if women would be women and let the men be the men God intended them to be. Fanny Wright was the epitome of a liberal, possibly, lesbian woman. Perhaps, she was one forerunner of that which now is the emasculated female.

> In 1829, American Illuminists sponsored a series of lectures in New York by English Illuminist, Francis "Fanny" Wright. She advocated the entire Weishauptian program.... Those in attendance were informed that the Illuminati intended to unite the Nihilist and Atheist groups with all other subversive

organizations into one organization known as Communism. This new destructive force was to be used by the Illuminati to foment future wars and revolutions.[99]

What most of the American public refuse to believe, and where they have buried their heads in denial, is that from the inception of our country to the present, 33rd degree Masons have participated in the Illuminati and other subversive organizations, with the intent and purpose of overriding our sovereignty.

These highly secretive organizations have been a shadow government within our government unknown to the populace, directing every move slowly, yet deliberately, to achieve their means. They are not interested in nationalism or separate governing countries and cultures led by the citizenry; but, plan to achieve one superior race built on their Luciferian idealism…a Utopia that would strictly be theirs. This, they have always falsely attributed to the Jews. This is to be brought about by their New World Order.

George H. W. Bush was the first president to openly espouse the "New World Order," which became a theme uttered by him during his entire term, then by Bill Clinton, and, more recently, G.W., who uses the term, globalism in its place. Globalism is the new word used to disguise this move for world government. When too many people began to understand the term, New World Order, the elitists modified it to globalism.

Mazzini and Pike

Guiseppe Mazzini and Albert Pike's relationship was diabolical...one could say "born in hell." Mazzini had organized the Italian Mafia. His choice to oversee the United States Illuminati was Albert Pike. Pike controlled the theosophical aspects of the Illuminati and Mazzini the political realm.

As we have seen before, Albert Pike was a rotten and despicable man with absolutely no character or moral values. He wrote the Masonic, *Morals and Dogma,* the name itself is deceptive. For, if one were to believe Pike's lifestyle was morally upright, they would be laboring under extreme delusion. Yet, many within our government have, and have erected a statue to him in our national capitol, Washington, D.C.

As is often the case, supreme intelligence is a gift misused for the devil. Such was the case of Albert Pike... a devoted occultist. Albert Pike was a genius who used his intelligence for evil. He was fluent, reading and writing in 16 ancient languages; and a devout admirer of the secret Hebrew cult of cabala...Pike served as head of the Ancient and Accepted Scottish Rite of Freemasonry, strategically placing the Illuminati's plans in place. Together, he and Mazzini made an extremely corrupt team. In a letter dated January 22, 1870, Mazzini wrote to Pike:

> We must create a super rite, which will remain unknown, to which we will call those Masons of high degree whom we shall select. With regard to our brothers in Masonry, these men must be pledged to the strictest secrecy.

Through this supreme rite, we will govern all Freemasonry which will become the one international center, the more powerful because its direction will be unknown.[100]

Salem Kirban, relates in his book, *Satan's Angels Exposed,* how Mazzini and Pike planned to overtake the world, by the use of subterfuge and secrecy within Freemasonry. Their scheme was to include revolutions and three world wars; two of which have already been fulfilled, murderously eliminating many Godly souls.

1) The first was "to enable communism to destroy the Czarist government of Russia,"

2) The second was to manipulate…."the governments of Great Britain and Germany to start a world war. Hitler, however, accomplished this almost single handedly;" it was promulgated by the two Illuminists that "Communism would then be in a position to destroy other governments and weaken religions. This also came to pass."

3) The Mazzini-Pike blueprint also called for a World War III. This would begin by firing up the controversy between Judaism and the Moslem world. They hoped that the Zionists and Moslems would destroy each other and bring the rest of the world into a final conflict. This Armageddon would bring complete social, political and economic chaos.[101]

The Pike-Mazzini blueprint to this day has been

worked out to with precision They received their directions from the same source, Lucifer, who was also the "author" of *The Protocols of the Wise Men of Zion,* and god of the Rothschild family.

Kirban wrote of these plans regarding the Third World War as early as 1980. Pike and Mazzini had received their instructions much earlier; and, we can see their implementation is underway.

How true. *"...evil men and seducers shall wax worse and worse, deceiving and being deceived."* (2 Timothy 3:13) These diabolical plans have all come about through subterfuge and deception of a few men who chose to serve Lucifer. They have had no idea that they have unwittingly been instruments in the hands of Almighty God to defeat His great adversary, permitting Satan to "hang" himself. In the process, many have laid down their lives for the cause of Christ, not knowing that their grace during persecution is a manifestation of the power of the cross and representative of the crucified One, living His life through them.

Believers should by all means renounce and separate themselves from the deceit of Freemasonry, or any other secret society, lest they, too, become enmeshed in the web of Lucifer's lies and the One World dictatorship.

CHAPTER NINE

THE ILLUMINATI
(Cult of the All-Seeing Eye)

As a cage is full of birds, so are their houses full of deceit: therefore they are become great and waxen rich. They are waxen fat, they shine: yea, they overpass the deeds of the wicked: they judge not the cause, the cause of the fatherless, yet they prosper; and the right of the needy do they not judge.

(Jeremiah 5:27-28)

One cannot discuss the Illuminati without looking into the world's elite families. We've already seen that this is a sinister group bent on world domination. Looking refined and cultured, it should be remembered, that looks are deceiving. For these elitists are nothing more than humanistic thugs under nice trappings.

These fiends have planned to gain control over every aspect of civilization. Their plans include control of all the world's monetary systems and corporations. They hide behind a multitude of secret organizations in their devious designs to rule the world. Their undercover operations have initiated wars, (for which they have funded both sides), and financial depressions. Their fear tactics control the minds of the unsuspecting through subliminal messages via the media. The Illuminati's body of followers intends to reduce the population by whatever means possible, including infanticide and genocide. This they have worked to accomplish by first "dumbing them down" to control them, body, soul and spirit.

> The Illuminati is divided into the drug/porn section, the political/business management section, the cult ritual section, global communications section, and mind control section...leadership...areas overlap....The three groups...entrusted with long-range plans are the Order of the Garter, Order of the Quest and Keepers of the Dawn...plans to bring in the New World Order are very detailed...their management and safekeeping have not been haphazard.[102]

Fritz Springmeier in his book, *Bloodlines of the Illuminati*, names the families that either by financial genius or by occult power are instrumental in development of the Order. Mr. Springmeier has done considerable research and has interviewed and deprogrammed many former Illuminati members.

> The Illuminati believe they are superior and have a right to rule over lesser men...One does not have to understand about...hidden Illuminati genealogies to have experienced the attitude of superiority of the aristocratic families that control the world. The pride of the aristocratic and rich families is well known to the world.[103]

Anyone who has made a study of ancient Babylonian or Egyptian worship soon finds the trail leads straight to, Catholicism, Masonry, and, of course, the Illuminati,. It is a continuation of the Gnostic teaching of Ancient Wisdom… a throw off of Nimrod's kingdom. The Illuminati/Masons use the All-Seeing eye as a symbol…it is the symbol of Horus, as previously mentioned.

> The All-Seeing Eye can be found on ancient buildings in ancient Chaldea, in ancient Greece, and in ancient Egypt…The temples in Arabia, back in the time when Moses had his black father-in-law Jethro, used the All-Seeing Eye to represent the false satanic trinity of Osiris, Isis and Horus of Egypt.

> This All-Seeing Eye pops up everywhere the Illuminati has been. In the Winder Palace Square in St. Petersburg, Russia, is an Illuminati All-Seeing Eye on top of a pyramid. You'll also see it in the old Mexican Senate Building, which is now a museum in Mexico City. You will find this All-Seeing Eye on the back of American one dollar bills and you will find the All-Seeing Eye was placed on Ethiopian stamps when a communist regime took power.[104]

As Springmeier researched the bloodlines and interviewed former Illuminists, he discovered that:

> The connections between Mormonism, Freemasonry and Witchcraft were extensive. Witches were told to join the Mormon Church to experience a high form of witchcraft. Mormonism was developed as a high rite of Freemasonry. Mormonism uses the traditional symbols of the Merovingian dynasty, for instance the bee.[105, 106]

The Illuminati/Freemasonry/Monarchy connection is inseparable. It is known that these three control the reins of the Mafia (originally organized by Guiseppe Mazzini), drug cartels, pornography and pedophile rings worldwide. Malevolence lurks deep within the Illuminati.

The Illuminati is composed of several bloodlines, each of whose families are members of Freemasonry and/or Skull and Bones, Council on Foreign Relations, the Trilateral Commission, Club of Rome, and, in some cases, all of them. The list of these organizations (some clandestine, others not) is quite lengthy. It includes many groups and orders, such as the Committee of 300, RIIA, the Pilgrim Society, Knights of Malta, B'nai B'rith, ACLU, and others; whose members either knowingly, or unknowingly, carry out the Illuminati's devious instructions.

> When the Prince of Wales, Richard of Bordeaux, was introduced to Parliament in 1377, it was made clear in the introduction by the Bishop of St. David that he was the ruler over Israel. People think that British Israelism is something new. The British monarchy has secretly considered them selves to be the descendants of King David for 2000 years.[107]

As of 2002, the following families were listed in the *Bloodlines of the Illuminati*:

- Astor
- Bundy
- Collins
- Dupont
- Freeman
- Kennedy

- Li
- Onassis
- Rothschild
- Rockefeller
- Russell
- Van Duyn
- Krupp
- Reynolds[108]

The principle overseers of these cryptocracies are based in Britain under the Order of the Garter. This Order's authority comes directly from the British monarchy. This fact is confirmed by the research and writings of Tim Cohen within his book, *The Antichrist and a Cup of Tea*; as well as the findings of Fritz Springmeier in his *Bloodlines of the Illuminati*. According to Springmeier:

> The Order of the Garter is organized into covens. It has control over all the heraldry of the world. Of course, heraldry is important to these elite families. The occult symbols they use on their crests are very meaningful to them.[109]

We will see in a future chapter, how Prince Charles' heraldry fulfills the symbolism of the Antichrist in Revelation 13. Few realize the evil that exists within the Illuminati, and especially its covering body, the Order of the Garter. No words can express that insidious evil adequately. To discover the extent of how deeply some of the people are involved and whom we might have thought to be on the up-and-up can be quite surprising and, sometimes, devastating.

One particular individual, Prince Charles, heir

apparent to the British throne, is deeply involved in the occult, as is the queen mother. Tim Cohen, author of *The Antichrist and a Cup of Tea,* confirms Springmeier's statement that the queen and Prince Charles oversee the Order of the Garter, composed of thirteen witches' covens under the queen and thirteen covens under the prince. With incontrovertible evidence, it should be noted that the highly honored and esteemed royal family is not Christian, as supposed, but actually in league with Satan.

> Great Britain is the mother country of Satanism. This is widely known by generational Satanists. Great Britain is the center for generational Satanism. Obviously then, whoever rules the United Kingdom must tie in powerfully with that Satanic power.... No wonder (people) like the Rothschilds wanted to make the world subservient to the British nation.[110]

Government Control

Illuminists maintain authority over world banking, including the World Bank and the Federal Reserve. The Federal Reserve is not a part of our government, as most believe, but is privately owned by the Rothschilds, and Rockefellers.

> The Federal Reserve bill was sneakily passed through Congress (and) in…1913…President Woodrow Wilson signed the bill into law. The Illuminati, particularly, the Rockefellers and Rothschilds, had usurped what remained of the government's financial power…The Fed…[111, 112]

1791: The Rothschilds get "control of a nation's money" through Alexander Hamilton (their agent in George Washington's cabinet) when they set up a central bank in the United States called the First Bank of the United States. This is established with a 20-year charter.

Within the first five years of the life of this central bank, the American Government will borrow $8,200,000 from it, and prices in the country will increase by 72%.[113]

This pattern of governmental borrowing has placed the United States under the domination of the Illuminati-controlled World Bank. As a nation, we now owe trillions of dollars to the money lenders,

When Thomas Jefferson was Secretary of State, he had this to say: "I wish it were possible to obtain a single amendment to our constitution taking from the Federal Government their power of borrowing."[114]

The Civil War was planned to divide and conquer this new nation by putting pressure on the South, who was in financial difficulty because the North had imposed heavy tariffs on the South so they could not buy from the Europeans. When European interests lost the South's trade, they stopped shipping goods to them. The South was then forced to pay more when they had less money to purchase European products. It was as if their life's blood as states had been cut off.

Whereas we have always been told the Civil War was over slavery, in reality it was over economics. The war was secretly planned and carried out by the Illuminati money barons, at that time mostly the Rothschild family.

When the South rose up against the North because of the inflated prices they were forced to pay on goods, the Civil War started. It was not over slavery. That, too, has been propaganda against this nation to divide and conquer. The propaganda has been quite successful, as this nation has prejudicial factions that still divide communities. Slavery in any form is not right, but this war was agitated to gain greater control over America and its trade.

> This is when the money changers saw the opportunity to divide and conquer America by plunging it into Civil War. This is confirmed by Otto Von Bismark when he was Chancellor of Germany (1871-1890), who stated, 'The division of the United States into federations of equal force was decided long before the Civil War by the high financial powers of Europe, these bankers were afraid that the United States if they remained as one block and as one nation, would attain economic and financial independence which would upset their financial domination over the world.'[115]

At the height of the Civil War, Canadian troops positioned themselves at our northern borders, and French troops in Mexico (in defiance of the Monroe Doctrine) stationed themselves at the southern border. Lincoln saw trouble and went to New York to apply for loans necessary to meet the defense costs.

> The Rothschilds had engineered the war to make the Union fail, and were not about

to save it now, so they instructed their American banks to offer loans at 24% to 36% interest.[116]

Lincoln sought counsel. He did not want to incur a heavy national debt. He needed to finance the war but was uncertain what to do. Colonel Dick Taylor of Chicago told him to get "Congress to pass a bill authorizing the printing of full legal tender treasure notes…and pay your soldiers with them and go ahead and win your war with them also."[117]

Lincoln succeeded in having $450,000,000 "greenbacks" printed. This made the United States our own "governing body" once again, but put the elitists in high gear. Later, shortly before his assassination, Lincoln told Congress:

> 1865: I have two great enemies, the Southern Army in front of me and the financial institutions in the rear. Of the two, the one in my rear is my greatest foe.[118]

Many leaders, throughout our history have undoubtedly been seduced by "set-ups" guaranteed to make them puppets of the Illuminati's greedy bankers. Men have been placed in compromising positions, not of their own doing, with threat of physical harm or death to someone in their family or to themselves if they did not comply to legislation ordered by the "shadow government." In this way, many good people have become unwilling partakers of the elitists' avarice.

Leaders in all walks of life have fallen prey to situational bribery. Bribes have been used in various ways to buy the votes of elected officials and pave the way for passage of outlandish laws their electorate would never have approved. If they attempted to expose these evil people or interrupt their plans; in some cases, they later have been found dead under strange circumstances. Lincoln and Kennedy are two, who were shot because they dared take a stand against the devices of these evil men. Many such instances like this have occurred, but they have all been quietly shoved "under the rug".

In the United States, maneuvers have been used to obliterate the Constitutional rights of its citizens by Executive Orders written by such men as Franklin Delano Roosevelt, Bill Clinton and G. W. Bush, to name only three of the presidents involved. These three have backgrounds which reveal their membership in cryptocracies and interrelation with the British monarchy.

It is nothing for Masonic/Illuminists to rob, kill or destroy, if it will pad their pocketbooks and give them control. These men are vicious and malicious. They have resorted to murderous means in the past and continue their ruthless advances to bring nations into debt by revolutions, wars, famine, whatever it takes to break a nation's economy and sovereignty. There is certainly "no honor among thieves."

For their evil deeds, they like to place the blame on the Jewish people. Even though there are many Jews among their ranks, they are not God-fearing Jews, but Judaizers...Zionists,[119] who have no love for their fellow man. They have joined hands with other hateful men, and follow the Ancient Mysteries and the Talmud, and serve their god...Lucifer. Below is only one example:

1943:   February 18th, Zionist, Izaak Greenbaum, head of the Jewish Agency Rescue Committee, in a speech to the Zionist Executive Council states, "If I am asked, could you give from the UJA (United Jewish Appeal) monies to rescue Jews, I say, no and I say again no!"

He goes on to state, "One cow in Palestine is worth more than all the Jews in Poland!"[120]

To speak against these forces of Judaism is near anathema. For the deceived believe if you do, you are anti-Semitic. However, Jesus during His entire ministry had a controversy with these particular Jews. Anti-Semitic propaganda has been developed to deceive and make the deceivers appear as "angels," when they are, in fact, despicably evil and anti-Semitic themselves.

God does have a chosen remnant, but we must not "cater" to just any one who claims to be a Jew. We must exercise discernment. They could be a member of a secret society, bent on destroying those who believe in God... but, members of the synagogue of Satan. When a person, Jew or Gentile, becomes a believer in Jesus, they become a "Jew," circumcised in heart with the attributes of their heavenly Father. These are worthy of blessing. As quoted before:

For he is not a Jew, which is one outwardly....
But he is a Jew which is one minwardly; and
circumcision is that of the heart, in the spirit,
and not in the letter, whose praise is not of
men, but of God.

(Romans 2:28-29)

CHAPTER TEN

SOLOMON'S SEAL

An evil and adulterous generation seeketh after a sign.

(Matthew 12:39)

Riches often cause men to forget God; that was the case with Solomon. His affluent lifestyle and apostasy from the Lord caused him to marry many wives of foreign gods. We have seen how the roots of witchcraft passed to different areas of the world through the scattering of the peoples and confusion of languages at Babel. These practices were highly forbidden of the Lord; but, as Solomon drew away from the Lord, his wives who followed ancient Babylonian practices influenced him.

Solomon, as history confirms, became the most prosperous king known; but, he entered into abhorrent idolatry and witchcraft with his wives' foreign gods, undoubtedly passed down through the centuries prior, from Babylon. As he chose the gods of his wives, he honored Ashtoreth, also known as Astarte (another name for Easter) and Milcom, also known as Moloch, or Molech. These required human sacrifice.

> *And the high places that were before Jerusalem, which were on the right hand of the mount of corruption, which Solomon the king of Israel had builded for Ashtoreth the abomination of the Zidonians, and for Chemosh the abomination of the Moabites, and for Milcom the abomination of the*

children of Ammon, did the king defile.

(2 Kings 23:13)

Did Solomon repent of his idolatry? We may never know. We do know that his kingdom was split after his death. The larger part of Israel was handed over to Jeroboam, and the two remaining tribes known as Judah went to Rehoboam, Solomon's son. It is not the kingdom split we are concerned with, but the seal of Solomon. During his reign, he changed his seal from the name of God, to the six-pointed star, or hexagram. The hexagram has strong occult connotations, of which Solomon must have been aware. Nevertheless, it took the place of the name of God he once used as his seal.

> The Encyclopaedia Judaiac has this to say: "It is not clear in which period the hexagram was engraved on the seal of Solomon mentioned in the Talmud (Git 68a) as a sign of his dominion over the demons, instead of the name of God which originally appeared on the ring."[121]

Composed of two interlocking triangles, the hexagram in Masonry depicts their Masonic motto: "As above, so below," a perversion of *"...on earth as it is in heaven,"* as in the Lord's Prayer. Wherever they have had an opportunity to pervert the Word of God, or God's commands, occultists have done so. This is true in the use of the hexagram, which many have come to believe is a God-given insignia. However, the name itself reveals it is not a good sign, but born of evil.

> The root word hex is defined as (1) an evil spell, (2) a witch (v.t. to bewitch). (Funk & Wagnall's Dictionary).

Hex (heks) n. Something supposed to bring bad luck: v.t. to cause to have bad luck: hexa—combining form meaning six. (Webster's New World Dictionary).

The word, "hexagram," describes a geometric figure of six sides. (American Heritage Dictionary).

Magen David

This subject is of importance because of Rothschild connections and their influence on Israel and future world events. There are those who believe the six-pointed star is a God-given emblem and identify it with King David, it is anything but that. Its use throughout Israel is, perhaps, one of the more subtle subterfuges of Satan, inasmuch as the star was used in ancient witchcraft rites centuries prior to David's kingship

> Among Satanists and witches, the double triangle, the Seal of Solomon, also called the hexagram, is of great interest. This seal, known as the Magen David of the Jews, is actually composed of two triangles, superimposed on each other. One triangle pointed upward represents the flesh or material matter and the male generative act; the other, pointed downward, signifies female sexuality and the spiritual plane.[122]

Is the six-pointed star Jewish, or did it originate at the time of Babel? While the Jews claim it as their national emblem under the title of the "star of David"; Muslims have referred to it as the seal of Solomon and believed it had magical powers. Muslims are not alone in their belief that the hexagram had magical powers, occultists the world over are in agreement, as are their Masonic counterparts.

>...it is reported that the six-pointed star or hexagram is not Jewish. They claim that the Muslims call it the "Seal of Solomon" with likely reference to magical powers which it is said the king had through his ring...it is stated that the term Magen David had no original connection with the hexagram, God Himself is called David's Shield.[123]

In attempting to trace the hexagram back to King David, there was one reference that seemed to connect David with the use of the hexagram; however, this was found upon a tombstone in Italy, after the death of Christ. Upon the tombstone was engraved a hexagram with the name David on it. It proved to be the grave of a writer, who had written a book called, *Magen David*. There is no other available indication of David ever having used a hexagram for his shield, or for any other purpose.

>The shield carried by King David on the battlefield was traditionally believed to be engraved either with the name of God or the Menorah, or Psalm 67.

>(One)...reference contends that there was a primary connection with the name David and the hexagram, and this was engraved on a tombstone in the 6th century A.D. in Italy which belonged to the astronomer and historian, author of a book called Magen David (1613), but any connection with King David (of Israel) may not have been intended.[124]

Scriptures in Amos and Acts indicate they made a "star" of idolatry to worship. Idolatrous worship is rebellion against the first commandment and angers Almighty God. It has always brought Jews under judgment, as it will any people, who repeatedly ignore God's commands. There is nothing that angers Him more than the worship of other gods, and judgment upon those He has chosen to serve Him is a certainty if they do.

> *But ye have borne the tabernacle of your Moloch and Chiun your images, the star of your god, which ye made to yourselves.*
>
> (Amos 5:26)

> *Yea, ye took up the tabernacle of Moloch, and the star of your god Remphan, figures which ye made to worship them.*
>
> (Acts 7:43)

The worship of these gods and their representative "star" first traveled from Nimrod's kingdom into Egypt, then from Egypt into Solomon's kingdom. These ancient worship rites are still practiced within the occult. There is further evidence that the seal of Solomon is in use within Masonry, identified with the square and compass of their organization.

> Perhaps most ironic, the very sign of the Jew in today's world—the six-pointed Star of David—is not really the historic symbol of Jewry, nor was it used as a religious sign by the Israelites.
>
> Construction workers apparently were digging in Ramle which is a town near Tel

125

Aviv in Israel and they found the six-pointed star imbedded into a mosaic floor which was about 1,200 years old. However, it was established that the floor was Moslem, not Jewish.[125]

What Solomon left behind was not only the division of the twelve tribes of Israel, but evidence of his idolatry. His foreign wives led him into the worship of the goddess Astoreth, otherwise called Astarte (meaning star). The six-pointed star or hexagram, which came to be called the "Seal of Solomon" when King Solomon took it upon himself, was the chief article of this pagan worship.[126]

The obverse side of the hexagram reveals the pentagram, a geometric sign, which is an outline of the Goat of Mendes, et al. These two stars, the five-pointed and six-pointed, each have great significance to the occult; and, they are used throughout the world in hidden symbolism only the initiated into the "craft" recognize. As the time is nearing for the appearance of the Antichrist, the Illuminati and other brotherhoods are becoming more and more open in their use of these "logos".

Of further note is a ritual performed in the Order of the Beast, or the OTO[127].

If one were allowed to peer inside an OTO lodge in Japan, Brazil, Israel or Texas, one might even see rituals performed by those possessing dual initiation in the related Order of the Beast known as the "Silver Star." Here one would observe a robed initiate perform the *Greater Ritual of the Hexagram, a ritual most Masons have never seen, in spite of the clear hints and references to the Kabbalah* in the writings of their own leaders, writings the average Mason never studies.[128]

When we discover the superstitions commonly held by occultists and Freemasons, we soon discover that these groups were responsible for many of the logos that we take for granted in our every day experiences. We have so readily accepted them that we fail to recognize their source may have come from something other than a man's good imagination, but rather from the influence of a satanic culture. One such thing is the "silver star," an emblem almost revered by Texans and law enforcement officers.

Omen of Evil

Within the occult are several rites that use the symbolism of the star. Not the least of these is Halloween. Halloween was earlier observed as a high holy day of the Druids. The quotation below shows early use of the hexagram, *not to be confused with the pentagram, also a satanic symbol used in occult rites.*[129]

> It emanates from the 14th century during the Dark Ages when the Druids would knock on the doors of the castles demanding the young maiden or princess for their sacrifices. If they were not given the maiden, they would paint a hexagram on the door to tell the others coming along that all should die in that household. If they were given the maiden, then a jack-o'lantern was put in the window to say they got what they wanted.[130]

The nation of Israel is God's chosen people. In light of the triangle, a favorite object of occultists, and the six points of the triangles, the "six within a six", or 666, quite possibly it's an indication that Jews have once again been marked by the cabalists of Ancient Wisdom belief for annihilation. The star on the Jews of World War II was an armband, emblazoned with a yellow six-pointed star. Those who wore it ended up in Nazi death camps.

Since research has not given any indication that the seal of Solomon came from a "Star" of David, we must wonder at Rothschild's influence over the nation of Israel. The seal of Solomon was their family shield, however, originally red.

> 1948…The flag of Israel is unveiled. The emblem on the flag is a blue coloured version of the Rothschild "Red Hexagram." It has a blue border at the top and the bottom, which represents the Nile and Euphrates rivers. This is put there to make the Jewish territorial ambitions very clear, an Israel in accordance with its biblical borders. This would of course mean the inclusion into Israel of Iraq, Syria, Jordan, Lebanon; and parts of Saudi Arabia.

> The use of the Rothschild Hexagram is disguised as it is referred to in the Rothschild media as a "Star Of David." However, it is clear to anyone with knowledge of esoteric symbolism that this Hexagram was used in the ancient mystery religions as a symbol of

"Molech" (described as a demon of unwilling sacrifice and also, interestingly, the name of the stone owl the elite worship at Bohemian Grove) and, "Astaroth" (described as the Lord Treasurer of Hell). Due to the fact it is made up of six lines, has six triangular sectors and six points, it is commonly regarded as a symbol of Satan.

So, to recap, the hexagram on the Israeli flag represents the number of the beast 666, it is an ancient representation of Satan....[131]

The colors of the Israeli flag are the same as those used by the United Nations, another arm of the Illuminati and its powerful elitists, whose families helped finance Hitler's Third Reich, among those wealthy barons, the Rothschilds. Their money has purchased great parts of Israel, which they control today, and they are known to have dictated their wishes to the Zionist Organization regarding the Jewish flag and other erstwhile ventures, all the time pretending to be "good" Jews.

Sixes and Sevens

Is it possible that once again the hexagram marks the Jews for a Fourth Reich annihilation, this time the Great Tribulation? Should that be the case, it will come on the heels of the Fascism that is making its way quickly into the United States and other regions of the world. Christians will also be marked for the extermination, of that we can be certain.

Seven appears to be God's favored number. It is

found throughout Scripture from Genesis to Revelation in several places, not the least being the Sabbath, the special feast days, the number of churches, etc. David would have known the implications of the pagan worship of the star. Although the pagan star could have been a counterfeit of the true, as some Jews are given to believe, why would they use the number six?

> *Here is wisdom. Let him that hath understanding count the number of the beast: for it is the number of a man; and his number is Six hundred threescore and six.*

(Revelation 13:18)

That man is the Antichrist, whose number is 666. Incorporated within the six-pointed star are three sixes. In Hebrew the number "six" is *vav*, which means "and." There is always something else when there is an "and." In this case, it means man without God. What a perfect definition of the Antichrist!

> The hexagram, or six-pointed star, certainly has three sixes. It contains a six, within a six, within a six: 666. (Count the sides of each triangle facing the clockwise direction, the sides facing the counterclockwise direction, and the third six—the sides of the inner hexagon).[132]

It is an indictment against believers that we have compromised with the enemy and taken little interest in discovering and/or removing ourselves from things God has forbidden for our protection and instead have accepted them as something so cute, sweet or beautiful. These beautiful things may lead us straightly into the enemy's camp, not discerning their evil source.

> The hexagram is really a most powerful symbol, to witches sorcerers, and magicians! The hexagram is used in all sorts of magic, witchcraft, occultism and the casting of zodiacal horoscopes. Because it has six points, and because it contains a '666', the hexagram is considered to be Satan's most powerful symbol...The first six is formed by the sides of each triangle facing the clockwise direction; the second six is formed by the sides of each triangle formed by facing the counterclockwise direction; the third six is formed by the sides of the inner hexagon.[133]

The future will not be bright to those who attribute good as evil, and evil as good. Those who have not known depravity will most readily accept a popular politician not knowing what is on their agenda. For the most part, each and every politician running for election at this time, regardless of the party, or country, has aligned themselves with the same occult system that ushered in Nazi Germany's Fascism, disguised as a socialist democracy. We should not be surprised if six-pointed stars are again placed as armbands on men, women and children marking them for destruction if they disagree with so-called "political correctness".

Texe Marrs points out another possibility for this occult symbol:

Geometrically and numerically (points, lines,

triangles) the six-pointed star translates into the number 666. Thus it is very possible that the six pointed star could become the Mark of the Beast, the Antichrist, as prophesied in *Revelation* 13.[134]

This is quite unlikely, however, we must not forget that trickery of any kind can be expected of these Luciferian followers and their future leader, Antichrist. As those before, who were marked for death in World War II, the occult's One World Order, plan to destroy all who attempt to defy them.

Before all of this takes place, it will appear fairly peaceful. During this time, those who fail to watch can be lulled into a false euphoria. Beware,

...for when they shall say, peace and safety, then sudden destruction cometh upon them... and they shall not escape.

(1 Thessalonians 5:3)

These are the times we are entering; and, if we are unaware of the prophesied path that lies in our future, living just for the day or the thrill of the moment, we may find ourselves wearing an armband with a star on it, marked for destruction. We must not be afraid, but discern and speak out against seducers, liars, and deceivers. History has always repeated itself. A majority seldom leads the pack, but a few wicked, deceived men and women who willfully use force, rule the masses.

In pre-World War II, those who rose against Hitler, were not fighting a regime, they were warring against the antichrist spirit, which rebellious monsters like Hitler chose to impose on God-fearing people and those who resisted his evil dictatorship.

The star, or hexagram, as has been shown, was not just a pretty logo to them. It was a symbol used within witchcraft denoting sacrifice. Human sacrifice is of little consequence to those in the higher circles of witchcraft, they have no regard for life. For the most part, they believe in reincarnation; and, therefore, it matters not to them if they "snuff" out another human being, as long as they are making an offering to their "god."

Perhaps, among the most zealous occult famiies are those whose choice symbol is the hexagram; this is the Rothschild family, undoubtedly, the most cunning, and ruthless of all. The hexagram, as previously shown, was their choice for the national logo for Israel. These people are not for Israel. Their aim is to install their man within the temple, when once again it is built. Speculations are, it will be done with British Monarchy and Rothschild money; and, although the perfect replica of King Solomon's Temple, will be strongly backed by Freemasonry.

CHAPTER ELEVEN

THE ROTHSCHILD FAMILY

For among my people are found wicked men: they lay wait, as he that setteth snares; they set a trap, they catch men. [27] As a cage is full of birds, so are their houses full of deceit: therefore they are become great, and waxen rich.

(Jeremiah 5:26-27)

The previous chapter relates the occult source of the hexagram. It is claimed to be the so-called "star of David," otherwise known as Solomon's seal, and the family sign of the Bauer family, who changed their name to Rothschild. Their family's financial prowess has been a force in the nation of Israel since its inception, wielding control over its leadership.

It's of utmost importance to know more about this highly influential bloodline of the Illuminati. Wealthy beyond anyone's wildest imagination, the Rothschild family has ruled the banking world for centuries.

If one looked on the backstage of history, he would find the House of Rothschild. They have indebted kings, manipulated kingdoms, created wars, and molded the very shape of the international world. Among the hierarchy of the Illuminati they are revered as a powerful Satanic bloodline. They are living legends.[135]

Of all the Illuminist families, the Rothschild family claims the dubious honor of being the only one to trace their roots back to Nimrod, the first type of Antichrist.

> Several of the Rothschild ancestors have been rabbis, and the early occultism of the family before they became Rothschilds is believed to have been in the form of Jewish Cabalism, Sabbatism, and Frankism. The House of Rothschild practices Gnostic-Satanism with a strong emphasis on Babylonian magic. The Rothschilds would not call themselves Satanists, but by our standards, considering their secret rituals and sacrifices, they are Satanists. According to their own secret family genealogy, which is recorded in a sacred, secret book, the Rothschilds are descended from Nimrod, the...Babylonian warrior.[136]

Even though they may make such an assertion, their roots actually go back to Askenazi Jews. At that time, they were known as the Bauer family. Their presumed lineage and deception can be attributed to rebellion against God. Whether the Rothschilds descended from Nimrod, were Ashkenazi Jews, or were true Jews is of little importance; their fruits have proven them to be evil through and through. Ashkenazi Jews were also known as Khazar Jews, and weren't Jews at all. Of Turkish-Mongolian descent, they eventually ended up in Russia.

> The riddle of those who say they are Jews but are not, and do lie may be explained by the fact that the men at the top tier of power in the

Synagogue of Satan organization have been proven…to be "Khazar Jews," also called, Ashkenazi Jews." The Khazars were a Turk-Mongol people…eventually integrated into the Russian Empire by the Czars. The King of Khazars forced his citizens, upon penalty of death, to convert to Judaism.[137]

Later, these Khazars, moved on to Eastern Europe. There in Europe, the Khazars—who *said* they were Jews and practiced a mystical and pagan form of Judaism—gathered in their own communities, keeping separate from those around them who they classified as Gentiles. The Khazar "Jews" considered the Gentiles to be racial inferiors. In fact, the racial inferiority of Gentiles was taught to them in their Talmud.

To this day, the Ashkenazi Jews, the heirs of the Khazar genealogical lineage, shun DNA tests. They want no evidence produced that will prove they are *not* Jews. They continue to lie and say they are Jews.[138]

The Rothschild family has proven they have no love for anything or anyone but their gods…Lucifer, power and money. Mayer Amschel Rothschild trained each of his sons to be ruthless financial schemers, whose only interest was to multiply their assets. The family heritage of financial acuity was passed from the father to his sons, then to their sons, from generation to generation.

These powerful bankers relate to faith in God as Cain related to his brother Abel. That they may be related *to the Jewish* people does not mean they have the Jewish people's best interest at heart.[139]

From their history, it is plain to see that they refused to worship the God of the Torah. Many historians believe the Rothschilds were of Jewish descent; only God knows the truth. If it is true they were related to Nimrod, their Jewish ancestry may have come from Mayer's mother. At the least, they are liars, deceivers and cut throats, people and God-haters.

> Mayer Amschel Bauer was a well-off coin trader in Frankfort. In front of his house hung a sign with the family's symbol, which was a red hexagram. The hexagram (also known as the Seal of Solomon, the Magen David, or the Star of David) is very occultic. It is used today as the symbol of Israel, but it is not Jewish.[140]

Although some would dispute their family shield to be an occult symbol, as was seen in the previous chapter, it can be traced back to Astarte, another pseudonym for Semiramis of Babylonia notoriety. Springmeier declares:

> Most Ashkenazi Jews of that time did not use surnames, instead they preferred the custom (like the Chinese) of using a symbol as the family identity. These symbols were sometimes used on signs outside Jewish houses as an address.[141]

True to the Rothschild nature, they chose the name "Bauer," which comes from the German term for farmer. The Bauer name continues today, but in the 1700s one man renamed his branch of the family after its symbol and address, the Red Shield, or the Seal of Solomon.

The family was retail traders at the time, and the name they took was another part of their trickery. They are bent, along with other Illuminati members, on destroying Christians and members of the Jewish race, that are not a part of their evil scheme to build a Utopia on earth.

Family Crest

In a previous chapter, we noted that Solomon apostatized from the faith and worshipped other gods, those of his pagan wives. The Bible has this to say about King Solomon:

> *And Solomon did evil in the sight of the LORD, and went not fully after the LORD, as did David his father. Then did Solomon build an high place for Chemosh, the abomination of Moab, in the hill that is before Jerusalem, and for Molech, the abomination of the children of Ammon.*

> (1 Kings 11:6-7)

Why would the Rothschild family choose to have the seal of Solomon as a family crest? Could it be that they could see an advantage of being identified somehow with King David and British royalty? The only thing clear about this is that the seal of Solomon, or the six-pointed star (hexagram), was a symbol used when sacrifices were made unto heathen gods.

The Rothschild use of the hexagram is proof they were not God-fearing. It is known that the hexagram is an occult symbol. The hexagram was also dedicated to Saturn, another name for Satan.

The Bauer's use of a hexagram as their family

sign points to their involvement in Jewish Cabalism. In fact, the six-pointed star was so significant to them that Mayer Amschel Bauer decided to adopt it as his new name— Mayer Amschel Rothschild...this was done to identify his family with occultism and the focus on Saturn (Astoreth worship) such as the Astor family, who are also a German-Jewish cabalistic family named after Astoreth.[142]

Zionism[143]

Mayer Amschel Bauer had five sons, which he strategically placed all over the continent of Europe. These men were taught high finance and learned how to use usury to the family's advantage. The sons and grandsons were taught the skillful art of fraudulent finance by Papa Rothschild. Over the centuries, his sons, grandsons and great-grandsons have proven to be financial geniuses...all the apples didn't fall too far from the tree.

> ...the House of Rothschild has been in existence and working in very strategic centers of the world, until today. They own banks and vineyards all over the world and colonies in Israel. Today they are indeed one of the most powerful and wealthiest families on this earth.[144]

The first Edmond Rothschild (others followed) was instrumental in acquiring the land of what was then known as Palestine (now Israel) for a homeland for the Jewish people. It seems that during the Crimean War, the Jewish people (a small community) were unable to get their needs met from any outside help. Edmond's father, James, took action by opening the James Mayer de Rothschild Hospital in Jerusalem. It is a fact that those involved in the Illuminati, or in Freemasonry, feel it necessary to do "good deeds" to balance their evil, so this good deed was one to balance the fraudulent business dealings they had. Jews fleeing Russia were given some aid by Edmond, but that aid barely scratched the surface of the needs of the people.

> Zionism is a massive subject indeed. In order
> to consider this development, it is necessary
> to go back to the very first known record of
> any attempt to occupy Zion.[145]

An entire tome could be written about the Zionists. Zionism came from attempts of several individual Jews to secure a homeland. They prefabricated lies through the centuries to make the God-fearing Jews and Christians out to be the real "enemy"; hence, those who worship their other gods or goddesses, steeped in the occult, twist everything. Their propaganda says it's a Jewish problem, and must have a solution. The holocaust of World War II was the "solution," killing millions to promote their anti-God cause.

This "mind control" misinformation was used by Hitler and is being used against God-fearing Jews and Gentiles again to put into place their plans; however, they are fulfilling end-time prophecy, unaware they are tools in the hands of Almighty God…the God they hate.

> At this point it is vital to ask the question:
> Are all Jews Zionists? The answer, of course,
> is no. In fact, many are opposed to Zionism.

Another question...: Are all Zionists Jews? The answer, of course, is no.

Are all who say they are Jews really Jews? For the answer to this question, let us hear from Jesus, Lion of the tribe of Judah: *"I know the blasphemy of them which say they are Jews, and are not, but are the synagogue of Satan."* (Revelation 2:9)."[146]

Throughout their lifetimes the Rothschilds have instigated stock market crashes and then provoked wars for monetary gain. They were oblivious to whom they backed or sold arms. They make arrangements as leaders among the elitists to stir opposing sides into hatred against each other, and, when war ensues, as arms dealers, they sell to both sides. Diligent in their devices, their ploy is always for financial benefit or more power. Then, when they have amassed larger fortunes, they use their wealth to control the poor, bribe governments and deceive the masses.

A Homeland

Dr. Theodore Herzl led the First Zionist Conference. It was Herzl who worked hard to bring about Zionism. He felt the Jewish people needed recognition and a homeland. He attempted:

> ...to get aid from Rothschild but was unsuccessful. He was unaware at the time that Rothschild had already established a lot of interests in Palestine and that he, Rothschild, was afraid that Herzl might upset them...(He) did not wish Herzl to destroy what he had set up...He wondered publicly how provisions

would be made for the 150,000 schnorers (beggers).[147]

Clearly, Rothschild (the first Edmond, called the "Father of Israel"), was not interested in the Jewish people; rather, he was more concerned with his own interests in Palestine. The trillions he had in his bank accounts could have easily fed 150,000 until they were settled. Their welfare was of little consequence to this ruthless, power-elitist. He chose rather to dominate through financial cunning and trickery, not realizing he was an instrument in the hands of God to fulfill His promises to His chosen people...the Israelites.

He first objected to establishing a Jewish homeland because he didn't feel the timing was right; he wanted the nation declared a nation first. Herzl won out, but later Rothschild's idea about the flag was accepted; and, a lone six-pointed star with the colors of the United Nations, adorns the Israeli flag today. Actually, Herzl would have liked several stars apparently surrounding the outside of a larger star with the name Lion of Judah in the center. His idea was replaced for the single star, picked by Rothschild.

The subject of the Zionists and the six-pointed star is many faceted, and all could not possibly be covered here. Apparently the development of the Jewish Homeland was because God saw the timing was right. Otherwise, Herzl could never have pulled off the plans for a homeland. That in itself was one of the innumerable miracles Israel has experienced since its inception. Herzl didn't have the financial backing, Rothschild did. The miracle was, that a man with unselfish ideals, as was Herzl, was able to secure the land for his people through earnest zeal and commitment. He was a righteous man, hating trickery, deceit and lies; and, God honored his honesty.

The message of the *"wealth of the sinner (being) laid up for the just"* can be seen in the manner in which the Rothschild's have had their financial hand in the initial structure of Israel's return; and, the subsequent building of national structures. For, unbeknown to them, their money is working to finance God's ultimate plan for Israel. The Rothschilds have considerable land holdings within the nation, and financially backed the erection of the Knesset and Supreme Court buildings.

God has had His way. He has used the wicked Rothschild money to fulfill His plans to restore the Jewish people to their homeland, and Israel has become a nation as prophesied. They have not as yet recognized it's not their power that will bring them through to victory over their usurpers. Through it all, God's hand can be seen using the wicked to establish those God intends to reclaim during the Great Tribulation.

Upon Herzl's death, another took his place as president over the Zionists. His name was David Wolffsohn. Wolffsohn knew which side his "bread was buttered on" and sought out Edmond Rothschild. Rothschild promised him help.

Connections

Rothschild was quite pleased to get Herzl out of the way; and, more than delighted when the person who later succeeded Wolffsohn was his collaborator and friend, Otto Warburg. Perhaps you will remember the name, as it is associated with the Federal Reserve fiasco and also the undertaking for the establishment of various church councils by the three partners in crime and deception, Rothschild, Rockefeller and Warburg. Warburg was from another "famous banking family."

> …Edmond #1 was a genius and a main figure in the creation of a Jewish homeland in Israel. He helped divide the world's oil between Shell and the Rockefeller's Standard Oil.[148]

Rothschild's "baby," the Illuminati, might have come to an abrupt end had the Bavarian government had their way. The Bavarians found the secret documents that exposed the Illuminati and that had been issued by Weishaupt and his associates; however, even then Rothschild money came to the Order's aid.

> …the Rothschilds had a major role in the Bavarian Illuminati. It is known that at least one of the sons of Amsel (sic) was a member…Amsel (sic) placed his sons in the major European capitals, where they each set up the principal banking houses. By their own intelligence service and their own news network they could outmaneuver any European government.[149]

Amschel Rothschild, though born in a poor farm

family, used his genius, patience and hard work to construct the House of Rothschild, known worldwide for its financial acumen. This diligence to hard work (albeit cunning, deceit and fraud) paid off handsomely and is the one thing for which Rothschild could be admired. His astuteness gave him the idea for a mail service that was more efficient than government mail and it delivered messages with such speed, the family was able to keep ahead of the governments of the countries in which they worked, keeping everything "under their thumb." It also worked well as a spy system to discover the financial plans of the royal families, and this enabled them to finagle their way into high places.

The Rothschilds are prominent members of the Bilderbergers, assuming some of the leadership of this vastly secretive organization that meets once a year under the cover of secrecy to plan world events. There are definite links within the Bilderbergers of the Illuminati and Skull and Bones' men concerning oil enterprises…Exxon, Shell and Standard, to name three.

Through privatization, the Rothschilds have taken control of many government-owned lands and services worldwide. They have accomplished this by amassing money through usury and sly covert actions with drug and sexual trade internationally. They are in league with Lucifer, and their demonic holdings are most visible in Israel. Their massive holdings have made them among the wealthiest families in the world; and, are only surpassed by the Royal family of England, whose holdings are said, including the crown jewels, to be in the trillions. The Rothschilds have said:

- "Give me control of a nation's money, and I care not who makes the laws". Mayer Amschel Bauer, father.

- "It isn't enough for you to love money, it's also necessary that money should love you." . Mayer Rothschild.

- "Permit me to issue and control the money of a nation, and I care not who makes its laws." Amschel Mayer Rothschild, son.

- "I care not what puppet is placed upon the throne of England to rule the Empire on which the sun never sets. The man who controls Britain's money supply controls the British Empire, and I control the British money supply." Nathan Mayer Rothschild, son.

Mayer Amschel Rothschild was trained to be a rabbi at the age of ten. He, however, apostasized and has wickedly controlled the lives of millions by his wealth. Through their extreme riches and ingenuity, the Rothschilds have succeeded in bankrupting entire nations. As early as 1823: "The Rothschilds (took) over the financial operations of the Catholic Church, worldwide."[150]

As previously discussed, Rothschild money financed the building of the Knesset and the Supreme Court in Israel, with "strings attached," of course. This edifice has geometric features that are Masonic and Satanic, including a pyramid inside a circle. A dot within a circle (as this would be viewed from above) is a choice symbol used by Illluminati/Masons. It's associated (symbolic) of the male penis within the female vagina; clearly, the All-Seeing Eye cult with all its many branches is sexually oriented. The symbol is revered as the sun-god; i. e., Saturn, or Satan, as well, and held in high regard by Satanists and witches.

With the Rothschild's background in mind, other strong connotations of occult origin are found throughout the Supreme Court Building. Including a cross, which can be trampled under foot. Outside on a wall near the garden is a plaque giving recognition to Rothschild. There is also an obelisk on the grounds.[151]

The obelisk, or "phallus" of Masonry and Egyptology, is situated near the Supreme Court Building. However, apparently unlike the Washington Monument, there is no reflecting pool nearby. In Washington, the obelisk's reflection is symbolic of the Mason motto: "As above, so below".

Israeli Holdings

Rothschilds are also owners of many other commercial holdings within Israel, among them the Hotel of Dan, which gives rise to the belief that they, like the Royal family of Britain, are interrelated with the tribe of Dan.

The tribe of Dan, as mentioned before, plays an integral part among the thirteen bloodlines of the Illuminati because of their connections to English royalty and the House of Rothschild. Prophetically, as noted before, Dan's heritage would serve Satan in the last days.

According to the testament of Dan, he

gathered his sons around him when he was 125 years old. Among the many things he had to say were these startling words: 'I read in the Book of Enoch, the Righteous that your prince is Satan....

Furthermore, in the apocryphal writing, Dan was made to say, I know that in the last days you will defect from the Lord, you will be offended at Levi, and revolt against Judah; but you will not prevail over them.

Finally, upon Dan's death, the writer concluded, "Dan prophesied to them...that they would go astray from God's law, that they would be estranged from their inheritance, from the race of Israel, and from their patrimony, and that is what occurred.'"[152]

The Rothschild's holdings contain much of the land around Caesarea, which they acquired around the 19th and early 20th century. This was purchased by Baron Edmond James de Rothschild. When Israel finally became recognized, they gave the holdings to the Caesarea Foundation, which is controlled by the Caesarea Edmond Benjamin de Rothschild Foundation. It is easy to see this family has their hand in "the pie".

The family can tie their lineage back to Dan. There is no doubt Dan's heritage will be instrumental in Israel's judgment. Their diabolical acts will surely bring about the Great Tribulation, or Jacob's Trouble, which will follow the Third World War, even now past the drawing board stage.

The end of the age when Jesus Christ puts a stop to idolatry and witchcraft practiced among those the world sees as beautiful and famous will soon come. At present, God is allowing the devil to have "his day," which will be short lived, and he and his followers will meet their doom.

Though it appears sin could get no worse, the world is becoming more lawless. The Antichrist is at the door, ready to make his appearance on the unsuspecting. The Church has remained in the dark and buried its head in the sand, because most don't want to believe we could be that close to the coming of the son of perdition; they're too busy playing games.

> For the mystery of iniquity doth already work: only he who now letteth[153] will let, until he be taken out of the way. And then shall that Wicked be revealed, whom the Lord shall consume with the spirit of his mouth, and shall destroy with the brightness of his coming: Even him, whose coming is after the working of Satan with all power and signs and lying wonders, and with all deceivableness of unrighteousness in them that perish; because they received not the love of the truth, that they might be saved.
>
> (2 Thessalonians 2:7-10)

When one is aware of the underlying schemes of Satan and his followers to bring about another major world war by leaning heavily on Luciferian doctrine, and subtly presenting their propaganda against the Lord, His people, and the Word of God, they will discern the times and take necessary precautions of obedience and seeking after truth, so as not to be caught in the strong delusion that will come to those who fall prey to the lies presented daily through the press. They will discern the times and take a stand against evil, even at great personal cost.

The Bible warns of the last-day apostasy. It is here. There is no question that the church is not what it once was.. Commercialism has in many cases overridden ritualism, neither of which are the embodiment of the true body of Christ, whose mark is humility.

Success has taken a form of godliness never intended by Jesus, or the early apostles. In some circles, if you haven't the funds here in the states for what appear to the masses to be necessities, then you are considered a failure, even if the necessities to them may be another expensive car, a summer home, or even a new cell phone. These are things we may have to learn to live without when the judgments begin to fall.

Baby-boomers have no concept of the words Fascism or Nazism. Most of them live for the day and are willing to have a part in a welfare state, as long as the government foots the bill. Others think the government is responsible for everything, and refuse to take personal responsibility for anything. This type of society is reminiscent of pre-World War II, when the people were primed to accept any one to rid them of social problems; hence, a Hitler.

It is open season for a man of sin to take the lead and bring swift destruction once again upon the innocent.

> The organized churches are guilty of both sins of commission and omission. In many instances, the church remained silent in the face of Nazi outrages. In other cases, the church actively aided and supported the Nazis. In still other cases, the church failed to counter erroneous teachings that eventually led to easy acceptance of Nazi doctrine.[154]

The church can no longer remain naïve about coming events; to do so will lead into deep deception like that which occurred during the Second World War, only this time with immeasurable death and destruction. During the Second World War, many who claimed the name of "Christian," allied themselves with Hitler, unaware that they were siding with occultists and ruthlessl men like the Rothschilds.

CHAPTER TWELVE

THE OTO (Ordo Templi Orientis)

For there are certain men crept in unawares, who were before of old ordained to this condemnation, ungodly men, turning the grace of our God into lasciviousness, and denying the only Lord God, and our Lord Jesus Christ.

(Jude 4)

Throughout history there have been men of degenerate minds...minds set upon evil, full of deceit, corruption and debauchery. When men, or women, refuse to accept the plan of God-given deliverance, and the only acceptable sacrifice, they become like those they serve. Like Cain, they become murderers; like Nimrod, despots; like Weishapt and Mazinni; cunning and devious; like Rothschild, ruthless and greedy. The results of rebellion against God and His promises are evidenced by following the pathways these men chose. Because of their twisted minds, they could not distinguish good and evil, and called evil good and good evil.

Reprobate, they had become unable to distinguish between soul and spirit; unaware of the eternal battle warring against their spirit, they give themselves over to fleshly works. Their souls darkened, their God-given talents were vested instead with satanic prowess. Their emotions, which they could have employed for mercy and compassion, became self gratifying; their intellect, which could have been used creatively to better mankind, became tools in the hands of Satan, enabling them to invent merciless weapons of destruction; and, their imaginations, became twisted with evil intentions, filled with suspicious, hateful and murderous thoughts …all of these bearing the fruit of the realm of the soul.

It was no misnomer when Crowley called himself "the wickedest man on earth. Aleister Crowley surely lived up to that infamous claim with his development of a gruesome Order, so secret few have ever heard of it, much less recognized that from its roots have emerged an alarming amount of heinous crimes against humanity.

Crowley, a Mason and a Catholic, was determined to develop a mass copied from Catholicism, into a Gnostic Mass composed of the Ancient Mysteries and the cabala of the Judaic Talmud. To do so, he stealthily moved among the clandestine organizations and watched their secret handshakes. When he became well-versed in their secret greetings, he used them to maneuver his way into their secretive gatherings to learn their hidden rites and incorporate them into the OTO.

In this way, the Ordo Templi Orientis (OTO) was developed. This sinister organization grew out of …"The Beast", or "666".

While other, cognate occult groups, such as Skull and Bones, certainly exert enormous power, none has the undisputable position in the world today which belongs to the OTO as the Judaically-anointed leader of the modern Beast Cult of the Kabbalah, and thereby of blood, control, deception, and death.[155]

Crowley held to the motto of the Hellfire Club, of which Benjamin Franklin[156] was a member. The motto was: "Do as thou wilt shall be the whole of the law." It can easily be compared with today's version: "If it feels good, do it." Without a doubt, this motto from Crowley's depraved imagination, was developed through association with his mentor, Lucifer, and writings within the Jewish Talmud.

> The OTO does not merely hint of occultism, but plunges, headlong into the very subjects the high degree Mason are told was reserved to the core of initiation. And at the core of these secrets is the embrace of contradiction, of the "elixir of life," and of the power of blood. Readers can judge for themselves how much of this gnosis is horrifying or simply sickening, the dark doings of the depraved.[157]

The Order is unquestionably linked to the hidden nucleus within Freemasonry. Let the reader not forget that it was Mazinni who first established the Italian Mafia and Albert Pike, the Ku Klux Klan. These men emboldened Freemasonry, and through their fiendish influence caused other murderous organizations to flourish.

The cult of the OTO is the essence, the innermost circle, of esoteric Freemasonry (although this fact will be denied by virtually every Masonic Lodge). But not only is the historical case for the genuineness of this claim too strong to ignore, inner circle members know the facts of the overlapping Masonic/OTO memberships, and keep these secrets to themselves.[158]

The average believer may be appalled at a message of such extreme human depravity as this being presented about the OTO. However, this naivete makes Satan's work much easier and the believer prey to his attacks. We must be on guard and not ignorant of his devices. Not to understand the intricacies of his tactics is to fall easy victim to deception. Subliminal messages have been among his strongest weaponry.

One of the founding tenets of the OTO is to shape and manage American popular culture symbolism, so that as a result we find a similar disguised satanic symbolism peering out from the edges of our consumer utopia. When it dawns on us that our participation in this commerce constitutes a form of demonic idolatry, we are told "not to worry," American culture is the enemy.[159]

. The unregenerate soul is easily entrapped by visual and/or subliminal messages which appeal to the sense realm of the soul, entering by way of sight, sound, smell, touch and taste. These were the gates to Eve's soul and used by Satan to manipulate her in the Garden of Eden. He has not changed his tactics.

The OTO can be considered among the most sinister Order of all secret societies, playing on the weaknesses and insecurities of man. Blood sacrifices are practiced in OTO rites; and, pedophilia, pornography, drug trafficking, slavery and murder encouraged.

Psychological Ploys

The voting public would be totally shocked were they to learn that these societies…especially where it concerns the OTO…play one political party against the other controlling both. The parties and their candidates are pawns in an antichrist movement intended to install Antichrist, but while doing so, plan to bring the United States into the One World Government through misguided, bribed, and/or deceived religious and political leaders.

One of the strong principles in use by the Illuminati/ Freemasonry leadership is that of G. W. Hegel. The Hegelian principle is simply this.

- Step One, *Create a Problem"*: Create it or take one that does not exist and built it up out of all proportion to its real importance.

- Step Two, *Publicize the "Problem"*: Make sure a story about this problem appears every day in newspapers, news magazines, radio and television. Hit it again and again in a "steady drumbeat" that soon has people who don't pay real attention to politics (which is the majority of them) clamoring for a "solution" to the problem.

- Step Three, *Offer a "Solution"*: A solution that takes away one or more of our rights and further undermines the constitutional protections we are all supposed to enjoy. One that involves higher taxes (to pay for this "solution", of course), and one we would not have allowed them to do without this previous conditioning of the public.[160]

These tactics were effectively used by Hitler before the Second World War; and, in countries where the news has been controlled, tyrants have been able to manipulate the people bringing them under their tyrannical subjection. As the reader was earlier informed, men like Rupert Murdock control the media of the United States. Of course, he is not the only one, but those in control may belong to any number of secret societies which are working together to reinforce the Hegelian Principle, conditioning the public to accept their devious schemes. The OTO makes full use of this principle, "...working secretly toward the alchemical[161] processing of humanity."[162]

Power brokers have used this strategy to their advantage for centuries. Perhaps the best and most recent example of how it works was the disaster of 9/11. There are those who believe this was an orchestrated terrorist attack. They could be right. There is much evidence to prove they are.

Notice how Hegel's principle was at work. The attack created a problem, terrorism. Then, the problem was publicized for days and months, and still receives media coverage. Lastly, a solution was offered...Homeland Security. Of course, without so much as a murmur or a batted eyelash, the public hastened to accept these security measures out of fear for their safety. Since this ploy works so effectively, it has proven beneficial to tyrants; they readily employ it with the backing of secret societies.

In light of this, it should be noted that a Masons motto is: Ordo Ab Chao, or Order out of Chaos. Now, let's take another look at 9/11. As the fear of terror attacks was highly publicized and the public continually advised of possible terrorist attacks, and still are; i.e., "Terrorist Alert: Elevated," through news strip announcements by major news outlets, the solution appeared evident (increase protection), Homeland Security.

Security measures through their encouragement, have been tightened and the people have accepted these restrictions to their rights out of fear, not recognizing the oppression that it is causing. Quite gradually more and more freedom is slipping away. This has always been the fate of people ignorant of Satan's devices, or who walk in rebellion toward God.

Examples of this trickery are the psychological media-inspired innuendoes which have pitted whites against blacks, male against female, and on and on. One only has to look at the historical facts and the radical change in the culture of its citizenry to realize something sinister has been afoot.

Strategies like these have been employed in past elections, the favorite candidate of the "shadow government" maneuvered into position through media "blitz". There is little difference between the Republican and Democratic parties. The powers behind the scene choose whom they deem to be the best "puppet" to carry out their ulterior motives in favor of their satanic New World Order, then, manipulate the mindset of the people to desire the choice of the power brokers, who had already made the decision behind closed-door meetings. .All of this subterfuge fits well into the Luciferian scheme, to which Crowley bore allegiance.

> Those who were close to Crowley knew that he was a control freak, and the worst type of proto-fascist. The OTO's appeal and one of the primary reasons it is so dangerous is that it is the heir to Satanic knowledge of human psychology. The fact is, Crowley's followers are found on the extreme Right, among people psychologically disposed toward royalism, authoritarianism, and elaborate ceremonies and pageantry.[163]

God's prophecies are being fulfilled and preparations underway for the installation of the Antichrist. While the Antichrist will be "pegged" as a man of peace, war is in his heart and his rule will bring devastation and genocide like the world has never seen, greater by far than the holocaust. The cryptocracies in an exerted effort to fulfill their plans for world domination, draft unwary souls into their fold, leading them down dark paths which can lead to bloody, human sacrifice.

> Brilliant and dedicated Freemasons…will end up in the OTO. There is really nowhere else for them to go, other than the Order of the Silver Star, which usually presupposes OTO membership, or if they are squeamish to the more conventional (albeit Luciferian) Hermetic Order of the Golden Dawn.[164]

Another reason, although veiled by intrigue, is the OTO and its obsession with the cabala.[165] The wicked, sexual perversion advocated by the OTO has its roots in the cabala and has made deep inroads in the lives of our youth, our school systems, mainstream television, and easily available pornography.

The Black Mass

The Vatican has secretly held OTO-type black masses for years. It should come as no surprise, then, that pedophilia, pornography, homosexuality and lesbianism are prevalent within the Catholic Church when black arts are practiced by the Jesuits, from which Weishaupt and many others received their teaching. It has been reported by Catholics themselves that 80 percent of the priests are homosexual. Rape involving young boys and nuns are frequent occurrences. It is rumored that murderous sexual rites have been performed within Catholic dioceses.

In one particular documented instance, Sister Margaret Ann Pahl, a nun who had threatened to reveal perverse practices by Father Gerald Robinson,[166] was brutalized and then sacrificed in a satanic black mass. This is only one of the mega sexual satanic rites performed against children and nuns by priests behind closed doors. When men take oaths to abstain from marriage, perversion will happen. The sex drive is the strongest drive known to man.

Lest we think Catholics are the only ones involved in perverse sexual acts, Protestants have skeletons in their closets, as well. Unbridled sex makes no distinction between Protestant or Catholic, white or black, male or female. More perverted acts are revealed each day, although, many have been kept undercover. These haven't been given as much publicity, and if they did, many of our politicians and highly-paid officials would no doubt be exposed; several have been known to frequent the Bohemian Grove, where satanic rites are held.[167]

Manipulated sex idols have long a long history in Hollywood. These idols, such as Marilyn Monroe, Britney Spears and others have frequently been victims of organized crime, and sometimes induced drug addiction, ending in suicide, or their lives snuffed out by sacrificial murderous rites. It may never come to light in some instances where these "stars" were found dead, whether or not their deaths were suicide or the result of ritual murder. It is believed that the death of Princess Diana was the result of such a ritual murder.

The OTO is quite capable of murderous rites. Whether those mentioned below were of that ilk is not known, but because of the character of the OTO, it is quite possible.

> If one were allowed to peer inside an OTO lodge in Japan, Brazil, Israel or Texas, one might even see rituals performed by those possessing dual initiation in the related Order of the Beast known as the "Silver Star." Here one would observe a robed initiate perform the *Greater Ritual of the Hexagram, a ritual most Masons have never seen, in spite of the clear hints and references to the Kabbalah*[168] in the writings of their own leaders, writings the average Mason never studies.[169]

Mass murders and crimes against humanity have been committed by those who have had association with, or have been members of the OTO. One such group was the Manson Family.

> Many books have been written about the "Manson murders," blaming Charles Manson's views on white racism and too many drug trips. His involvement with the Solar Lodge, however, is less well known. The successor to Parsons' Agape Lodge in Pasadena was located in southern California and numbered among its adherents a young man named Charles Manson.
>
> Manson was acquainted with the *Book of the Law* and its solid, literal basis for ritual murder...Mason may have read these words:

"Worship me with fire & blood...let blood flow to my name...Sacrifice...a child...Mercy let be off: damn them who pity! Kill and torture; spare not; be upon them!"

Whatever the case with Manson, Satanic Ritual Murder exists and can also be called Masonic Ritual Abuse and Mind Control experimentation as conducted by the so-called intelligence community, as the infamous MK-ULTRA program of the CIA, in which drugs, psycho-surgery, lobotomy, electro-convulsive shock and hypnosis were tried on various "patients."[170]

Our youth are ushered into witchcraft through Harry Potter books and other paraphernalia, among them, the Ouija board and Tarot cards. Strong evidence as to the occult's direction in the 9/11 attack was evidenced by the face of Tarot cards before the towers were destroyed. Tarot cards depicted two towers being blown apart; the enemy unafraid to announce his diabolical plans. At one time, these items were considered "off limits" and taboo; however, they are receiving popularity, a sign the apostasy is increasing.

Crowley developed the Tarot cards. The cards seem to attract youth, who seek to learn where an OTO Lodge is meeting. They enter New Age bookstores with the intent of buying the cards, or getting a particular Crowley book, which gives instruction as to how to make initial contact with the OTO.

This method continues to be one doorway for many youth into the OTO. I recently witnessed two young bookstore employees sorting the Tarot decks behind the glass case in a major chain bookstore; upon fingering the OTO deck, the young girl said, "I love Crowley—Crazy Crowley, crazy Crowley, he's so crazy," like a hypnotized parrot.[171]

These Tarot cards lead their adherents into perversion and the heinous crimes taught in the cabala. The cabala gives information only a degenerate would care to follow, but Crowley has encouraged men and women to worship the devil, and their degeneracy is the natural outcome.

The OTO is technically correct in explaining away any OTO requirement of worshipping the devil *under the name of Satan* but obviously...Crowley's writings are a potent endorsement of the practice.[172]

Anyone in the least bit knowledgeable about the occult knows that the Goat of Mendes, (sometimes pictured within the five-pointed pentagram) is "...a goat-headed figure called Baphomet."[173]

In the OTO's weekly Gnostic Mass, worshippers chant, "And I believe in the Serpent and the Lion, Mystery of Mystery, in His name Baphomet." After consecrating the elements in the Gnostic Mass into the "Body and Blood of God," the OTO priest genuflects and strikes his breast. The power of Baphomet is then invoked upon the worshippers present with the words, "O Lion and O Serpent that destroy the destroyer, be mighty among us."

This is said three times in place of the traditional *Agnes Dei (Lamb of God) portion of the old Catholic Latin Mass...the elements are adored as if they were God, and equated with the Lion and Serpent, who in turn is Baphomet; i.e., Satan.*[174]

If the above is difficult to believe, then you will find it more difficult to accept the further works of the OTO. Their gory rites have been somewhat unveiled recently, revealing the dark side of their particular rendition of the occult. It is, however, true that many kidnappings, gross murders and serial killings can be directly linked to the rites approved by Aleister Crowley for the OTO, but which came from the Ancient Wisdom of the cabala.

The roots of these pedophiliac practices, however, are not the Great Beast himself, nor even the OTO. The Cult of the Beast is an important modern branch from a much older tree. We must look back, past the incomplete initiation given to occultists through the centuries by their tutors and masters, to discern the roots of institutionalized sodomy of children...The roots of pedophilia, at least as far as the West is concerned, lie in the secrets of the Talmud. This provocative statement is not difficult to verify today, thanks to the accurate translation of a partial edition of the Talmud in English translated by Adin Steinsaltz.[175]

Believers are incredulous at such teaching; however, most live in denial as to the sign of the times, and have for centuries refused to recognize the danger of Masonry and its fraternal Order, the OTO. Both include many of these ancient rites, stemming from the Judaic Talmud and its "laws", which advocate pedophilia.

> Sanhedrin is a portion of the Talmud named after the rabbinic tribunal which sentenced Christ to death. In Sanhedrin 54b we read this argument: "…whoever can perpetrate sodomy can also be the object of sodomy… If a boy under the age of nine perpetrated sodomy upon an adult, the adult is not liable for punishment, for the intercourse of a boy under nine years of age is not legally an act of intercourse."[176]

This kind of writing could only have come from depraved minds, perverted by demons. It is no wonder their teachings and traditions led to the death of the King of kings and Lord of lords. Their writings could have been inspired by no other than Lucifer. Their adherents have absolutely no respect for children of any age, and use them to gratify their lust.

> Interestingly, the Jewish Talmud legitimizes sex with girls under the age of three and justifies it in the Mishnah of Kethuboth 11a, because, apparently, according to the Jewish Rabbis, it is like putting your finger in the baby girl's eye, and just as tears come to the eye again and again, so does virginity come back to the baby girl.[177]

There are those who think just because an individual is a Jew he must be blessed, or lose the blessing of God. To bless the kind of evil as found within the Talmud and those who adhere to its principles is cooperating with Satan, be they Jew or Gentile.

> It should be noted that…(Heimbichner) is in no way claiming or even implying that every OTO member is necessarily a pedophile. Many in the OTO are no doubt opposed to pedophilia, though on what grounds it would be difficult to say, given the license Crowley bestowed upon virtually every imaginable form of what until recently was diagnosed as clinically insane perversion.[178]

Teaching such as this found in the Talmud and the cabala have encouraged secret societies like Masonry, the Illuminati, OTO and others to exist. Among those associated with Christiandom today are men and women who are Jews, and/or of other faiths, but do not consider Jesus their Savior. The body of Christ should take care to discern between the true Hebraic Jew and the pseudo Jew, the true Christian possessor as opposed to the Christian professor. History is about to go full circle…persecuting true God-fearing men and women, because men love darkness rather than light, because their deeds are evil. (See John 3:19)

CHAPTER THIRTEEN

THE ANTICHRIST

*Neither shall he regard the God of his fathers,
nor the desire of women, nor regard any god:
for he shall magnify himself above all. But in
his estate shall he honour the God of forces:
and a god whom his fathers knew not shall
he honour with gold, and silver, and with
precious stones, and pleasant things.*

(Daniel 11:37-38)

As has been shown, a web of evil lurks hidden from sight within most governments and organizations. These secret societies, which appear as legitimate "clubs," have among their membership rolls individuals who consider themselves vastly superior to others. Demonically led, these men and women are intent on building a Utopia under the backing of their overlord, Lucifer.

In our own government, this core group considered the "shadow government" is unseen; but, pulls the strings of both political parties to conform to elitist ideology. Most of our presidents have been puppets in their hands, swayed by the influence of affluent and powerful money barons. Another striking, undeniable fact is that twelve of our presidents were blood-related to the Crown, which has exerted their influence on these men in an effort to reclaim the United States under the British Commonwealth.

An aspect of this scenario is the European monarchy and their position in this bizarre structure. The Royal family

169

is highly esteemed and believed to be above reproach by some. Looks and actions can be quite deceiving. Those who idolize the monarchy may do so without questioning their character or lifestyle. As Adam Weishaupt aptly put it: "Oh man, what can you not be brought to believe?"[179]

The royal crowns of Europe claim Merovingian descent, which can be traced back to the tribe of Dan. The British maintain they are from the bloodline of King David. Queen Elizabeth's genealogy chart[180] affirms this, linking her to the tribe of Judah; however, their ancestral ties with the tribe of Dan are equally as strong.

As Fritz Springmeier relates, British Israelism (another cult) is not new, but has long been the belief of those within the British Commonwealth. The doctrine believes the citizens of Britain and the United States are actually Israelites, supposedly from the tribes of Ephraim and Manasseh. This erroneous doctrine was strongly promulgated by Herbert W. Armstrong's cult. After his death they acknowledged it as false, and now claim to have repented turning from their error.

Intermarriage between royal families and the popery were commonplace before celibacy was introduced to Catholicism. Royalty, wealthy beyond words themselves, have strong connections with other extremely affluent occultists, those who rule the International Monetary Fund.

Adolf Hitler, Henry Kissinger, King Juan Carlos, Karl Von Hapsburg, Maitreya, Javier Solana, *ad infinitum* have been nominated at one time, or considered to be the Antichrist. Though some may think the Pope belongs in this lineup, the scriptures predict a false prophet, who will undoubtedly head the religious New Age Movement, giving homage to the Antichrist.

> *And I stood upon the sand of the sea, and saw a beast rise up out of the sea, having seven heads and ten horns, and upon his horns ten crowns, and upon his heads the name of blasphemy. And the beast which I saw was like unto a leopard, and his feet were as the feet of a bear, and his mouth as the mouth of a lion: and the dragon gave him his power, and his seat, and great authority. And I saw one of his heads as it were wounded to death; and his deadly wound was healed: and all the world wondered after the beast. And they worshipped the dragon which gave power unto the beast: and they worshipped the beast, saying, Who is like unto the beast? Who is able to make war with him?*
>
> (Revelation 13:1-4)

Satan was a seducer, liar, deceiver, and a murderer from the beginning. His subterfuge could cause Christians to believe the Antichrist to be one particular individual, when he has an entirely different individual in the wings offstage. There are many who believe they will not know who the Antichrist is before the rapture. This doctrine is quite deceptive, as God's Word states otherwise. Scripture is clear that he will be revealed after the "falling away," or apostasy, of the church and not before:

> *Now we beseech you, brethren, by the coming of our Lord Jesus Christ, and by our gathering*

together unto him, that ye be not soon shaken in mind, or be troubled, neither by spirit, nor by word, nor by letter as from us, as that the day of Christ is at hand. Let no man deceive you by any means: for that day shall not come, except there come a falling away first, and that man of sin be revealed, the son of perdition.

(2 Thessalonians 2:1-3)

According to Revelation 13, the wise will know who the Antichrist is by the number of his name. *"Here is wisdom. Let him that hath understanding count the number of the beast: for it is the number of a man; and his number is Six hundred threescore and six."* (Revelation 13:18) Given below is a partial list of the criteria the Antichrist must possess:

- Will be capable of speaking great words (Daniel 7:20; Revelation 13:5).

- Will look more stout (or great) than his fellows (Daniel 7:20; 8:23).

- Will be a military genius (Daniel 8:24; Revelation 13:7).

- Will be an economic genius (Daniel 8:25).

- Will be a tactful diplomat capable of gathering people together to unite in action alongside him (Daniel 9:27).

172

- Will, ironically, be seen as a peacemaker initially (Daniel 8:25; 9:27).

- Will be exceedingly arrogant and self-worshipping, whether it seems so initially or not (Daniel 8:25; 2 Thessalonians 2:4).

He will despise both Jews and Christians, which will not, in all likelihood, be outwardly apparent when he first rises to power. He will, instead, appear as a man of peace.

Tim Cohen, author of *The Antichrist and a Cup of Tea*, has thoroughly researched Prince Charles and has come to the conclusion that he is the Antichrist. It is a certainty that Charles fits the above criteria, with perhaps only one or two exceptions. However, before we discuss Prince Charles and his qualifications for this despicable position, let us identify some other candidates:

Maitreya designated by Benjamin Crème as the "Christ." Maitreya meets quite a few of the criteria, while missing in others. He is from the Far East and has scars in both hands. He dresses in white robes and has been considered a healer and man of peace.

Within Mexico, the Philippines and strong Catholic countries, flagellation is practiced. Men, to appease their "lord," purposely have been nailed to a cross. Maitreya could have received his scars in this way. He does, however, exude EVIL! There is a dark, heavy presence about him, even as he appears on the internet.

Juan Carlos has the dubious right to the title of Antichrist because he is known for his expertise in sports and politics. He is an OTO/Catholic and bears the title of King of Jerusalem because of his Merovingian bloodline, and he is the king of the tenth nation to join the European Union. He is an extremely wicked man. It has been reported he has worked inconspicuously behind the scenes at the peace talks. Carlos is known to keep quietly abreast of all that goes on in world affairs.

Karl von Hapsburg (also spelled Habsburg) has the right of title, King of Jerusalem as well, by the Merovingian bloodline. Karl's name, according to J. R. Church, can be numbered as "666," using the following system:

1	2	3	4	5	6	7	8	9
A	B	C	D	E	F	G	H	I
J	K	L	M	N	O	P	Q	R
S	T	U	V	W	X	Y	Z	

The value of all letters are added together.
Example: K - 2; A -1; R - 9; L - 3. 2+1+9+3 = 15.

 Then, as all double digit numbers, are combined into a single digit number: 666.

KARL	von	HABSBURG
2193	465	81212397
15	15	33
6	6	6[181]

Javier Solana is another prime candidate as head of the European Union's ten-nation military alliance and former head of NATO. He, too, is heir to the title King of Jerusalem by bloodline, although not by royal bloodlines. His last name means "Sun." The occult worships the sun god...by his numerous names...all of which point back to Nimrod. The sun god is known as Saturnia, or Stur.

The Clintons, both Bill and Hillary, could also be considered candidates, because their names, as individuals, can each be calculated to 666. This is true of others within the New World Order, but only by arriving at their "number" in a singular and often contrived manner; as were the Clintons and Henry Kissinger, for example.

The Pope has been mentioned as a possible candidate. It is more likely that he will be the false prophet, overseeing the New Age, One World Church.

Here is what Alexander Hislop, author of *The Two Babylons,* has to say:

> The name of the system is "Mystery" (Rev. xvii. 5). Here, then we have the key...We have not only to inquire what was the name by which Nimrod was known as the god of the Chaldean Mysteries. That name, as we have seen, was Saturn. Saturn and Mystery are both Chaldean words....

As Mystery signifies the Hidden system, so Saturn signifies the Hidden god. To those who were initiated the god was revealed; to all else he was hidden. Now the name in Chaldee is pronounced Satur; but, as every Chaldee scholar knows, consists only of four letters, thus---Stur.

The name contains exactly the Apocalyptic number 666.

$$S = 60$$
$$T = 400$$
$$U = 6$$
$$R = 200$$
_____

666[182]

In addition to the numbering of "STUR" are the letters which appear on the Pope's miter. These letters are the Pope's title, "VICARIUS FILII DEI."

V.....5	F.....0	D...500
I... 1	I......1	E......0
C...100	L...50	I.......1
A.....0	I... 1	
R.....0	I......1	
I......1		
U....5		
S.....0		
Totals: 112	Totals: 53	Totals: 501[183]

Added together these totals equal 666. Therefore, the Pope of Rome has two individual ways to arrive at the number 666...the number of a man, or the Antichrist, but is missing in other criteria.

With world events fulfilling the prophetical warnings of Matthew 24, Luke 21 and Mark 13 of the catastrophic days prior to the Lord's appearing, and with the warnings of the epistles clear and emphatic, as believers we are to "watch and pray," alert to any deception prevalent on earth.

There are many things yet to be accomplished: 1) The Third World War prophesied in Ezekiel 38-39, followed by seven years of clean up, and the leveling of the temple site for the restoration of the temple itself. Many believe the Antichrist will plant his feet on the demolished Dome of the Rock before the temple is built. All this remains to be seen.

Solid Evidence

Prince Charles meets the above criteria and more. He has an extensive background in every possible field of endeavor…religion, military, business, science, homeopathy and ecology. Without reservation, he has been instrumental in overseeing and initiating various foundations and organizations.

Tim Cohen has made a thorough investigation of every aspect of the prince's life. After reading his book and research, it is extremely difficult to believe that Charles is not the Antichrist. The evidence Cohen presents is overwhelming. As an example: No other coat of arms is like his, which, as in all heraldry, is protected by international law. His sons' heraldries are not even close to the Revelation 13 symbolism. Cohen has compared the symbolism of the prince's coat of arms to Revelation 13, and it fits perfectly.

1) Feet of a bear
2) Mouth of a lion
3) Power and authority of the dragon (the nation of Wales' flag and logo is that of a red dragon...his seat of authority)
4) A unicorn with a human eye
5) The restraining chain
6) Seven crowns (heads)
7) Ten horns (shown by smaller lions on the crest)

Charles' name "...both in Hebrew, Greek and English (Prince Charles of Wales), scripturally calculates to 666."[184] In addition, it is the opinion of most who have studied the New World Order that the Antichrist will arise out of the revived Roman Empire, which encompasses Europe. Prince Charles "... has requested to be made the King of Europe."[185] With ties universally, he could easily rise to this position; and, utilize the United Nations to further world domination.

His involvement with worldwide corporations is phenomenal. He has proved to be a leader with great ease and acumen, gaining the respect of CEOs everywhere. Financially, he is no slouch either, as he has joined hands with the World Bank, keeping a close eye on the International Monetary Fund; and, as a result, the money barons, which include the Rothschild family.

Charles' understanding of politics is possibly exceeded only by his involvement in, and spiritual acceptance, of virtually every known religion in the world. Although, his princely title has afforded him leadership over the Anglican Church, he has participated in a variety of religious rites in virtually every culture, easily adapting to their cult or occult doctrines. He is widely venerated in some places by those who consider him their "messiah." Only here in the United States have we heard little of his prowess in virtually every field of endeavor, and look casually upon him as somewhat of a "wimp".

Of great interest is his leadership over Freemasonry. The monarchy's roots go deep into this covert organization. The United Grand Lodge of England is considered to be the "mother" lodge over Freemasonry throughout the world, bringing John Daniel of *Scarlet and the Beast,* to believe that this decidedly strong religion (as it worships a god) is the "Mother of Harlots", spoken of in Revelation 17. This is noteworthy in the fact that Catholicism has lost much of its clout in the past few years; and, as shown before, the Rothschilds have gained control over the money of the Catholic Church.

Charles' has perfect legitimacy to the title of grand master over the English "mother" lodge; and, in this position installed the Duke of Kent who now holds the highest ranking place within Masonry. However, lofty this place of authority within Masonry may be, the Duke of Kent is still subservient to both the Queen and Prince Charles.

Charles received his *"...power, throne and great authority"* literally from the red dragon, or Satan"[186] as Prince of Wales, (whose national symbol is the red dragon). This, as previously shown, connects him with the description of the Beast in Revelation 13.

Prince Charles' "...media exposure has already exceeded every other man in history"[187] since his birth, nine months after the birth of Israel as a nation, November 17, 1948.

Anyone "googling" the web for "Prince Charles, Savior of the World," will see a bronze statue of him complete with "angel wings" and masses of depraved souls at his feet. Could this not be an omen of things to come? He has joined the Muslim faith; perhaps, because of his ecumenical leanings and his desire to be the "guardian of faith," which title was given to him when he underwent... ceremonies necessary to become a Muslim by the name of 'Abdus-Salem Hafidh ad-Deen," which means "The Guardian of Faith."[188]   He is highly esteemed among Muslims. For this reason, according to Mr. Cohen, there is speculation among "...Islam's top Muslim clerics...*that he intends to become the leader of the Muslims.*"[189]

Notice, Prince Charles does not say "*the faith.*" This makes quite a statement. His lineage unites him with most every nationality; therefore, he is considered to have Syrian blood and related to Antiochus Epiphanes...things believers look for when attempting to solve the "riddle" of the Antichrist. His Asian blood, for instance, is linked with Genghis Khan.

Of the cryptocracies, possibly the largest umbrella over all of them is the Order of the Garter. This deep-seated witchcraft cult operates under cover of the British monarchy. The world has been led to believe that this

Order is for the purpose of knighting well-deserved individuals...an overt deception. As overseers of this Order, Queen Elizabeth and Prince Charles are said to have under their leadership, thirteen witchcraft covens apiece, and those thirteen covens have thirteen witches, each participating in their rituals and embedded within a number of evil societies.

> The Order of the Garter is organized into covens. It has control over all the heraldry of the world. Of course heraldry is important to these elite families. The occult symbols they use on their crests are very meaningful to them.[190]

Mr. Cohen has taken great pains to discover the truth about Prince Charles, and we, as believers, should not scorn his findings in unbelief, but seek to discover the truth for ourselves. There can hardly be any doubt with the incontrovertible evidence Cohen presents, that Prince Charles is the man of sin. Only those who refuse to investigate the overwhelming documented proof would continue to question his findings.

During research for this book the writer looked up the meaning of the name "Charles". It means "man or strong man," and is just one more, tiny link identifying him with Revelation 13:18, which says, *"Here is wisdom. Let him that hath understanding count the number of the beast: for it is the number of a man; and his number is Six hundred threescore and six."*

(Revelation 13:18)

Knowing Prince Charles is the rightful overlord of British Freemasonry, is an overseer of the Anglican

Church, and a convert to Islam, it is plausible that he will one day, in the not too distant future, be revealed as the Antichrist. We are not saying here that he is the Antichrist, only that it is quite plausible. Whoever the Antichrist is, his followers will, in all likelihood as they already have with Prince Charles, call him "the Christ", which means "messiah", "savior", or "anointed" one.

Placing all faiths under one "mother" church for unity, connection, and "peace" will greatly appeal to the spiritually ignorant, or deceived. The false prophet, whether out of Roman Catholicism or from another source, makes no difference; but, the miracles performed by this prophet will direct a Jesus-denying populace to worship the Antichrist as the man of peace, believing him to have all the answers to the world's problems.

A news release was sent out recently regarding Prince Charles. Quoted are parts of an article taken from David Bay's, Cutting Edge Newsletter, dated January 4, 2008.

> ...Prince Charles will be speaking to an energy conference 7,000 miles from London through a hologram! This fact should immediately cause Christians to sit up and take notice, for two very important reasons:
>
> 1) The New Age plan for Antichrist is to have him appear to peoples all over the world simultaneously through a hologram broadcast from outer space

2) Prince Charles is from the House of Windsor, which we believe will likely be the place from which Antichrist will arise (See "Antichrist and a Cup of Tea" DVD, by… Cohen). If the Illuminati can bring about the World War III which will produce Antichrist in the next several years, he will likely be Prince Charles….[191]

The reason Mr. Bay's article commands so much interest is that it is the imagery of the Beast the false prophet will cause people to worship. The imagery could well be a hologram. A hologram image can be seen by the masses far and wide via satellite, and appear to be someone talking to them in person.

> *And he had power to give life unto the image of the beast, that the image of the beast should both speak, and cause that as many as would not worship the image of the beast should be killed.*
>
> (Revelation 13:15)

To conclude this chapter, it is suggested that the reader continue to watch the events transpiring around the English monarchy, and notice the increase in publichity about them that has been coming forth in more recent months. It remains to be seen whether Charles is the Antichrist; however, those who wonder how such a "wimp" could possibly be the man of sin, the scriptures make it quite clear that the Antichrest will be killed and brought back to life again, his body, persumably possessed by none other than Satan.

Atrocities performed against humanity by other antichrists will in no way compare with those of the "... *prince that shall come...*". (Daniel 9:26) That time is fast approaching, If the "prince" is already in place just waiting for the right time, world events are quickly propelling him into place.

CHAPTER FOURTEEN

THE GRAND FINALE

He that believeth on the Son hath everlasting life; and he that believeth not the Son shall not see life, but the wrath of God abideth on him.

(John 3:36)

The greater share of the population is unable to think for themselves. Locked into the pretense of television soap operas, sports events, or mind-capturing fantasies, they have been deluded by psychological ploys aimed to throw them off guard and squarely into the enemy's camp.

Unable to distinguish between good and evil, right or wrong, they are intent on pleasure, amassing wealth, or seeking man's approval in one way or another, forgetful that their understanding of God and His purposes brings peace of mind in the middle of chaos. They are shrouded in darkness, unaware that Jesus is the Light of the World.

In nations, tyranny follows disobedience and rebellion against the Lord. His judgments do not always come immediately, as He is merciful and slow to anger. But, there is a time when God will say, "That's enough!" Whether judgment upon a nation or an individual, there is nothing quite so devastating as falling into the hands of an angry God.

The children of Israel had been under the spiritual

guidance and leadership of Samuel but, they wanted a change. That's the cry of the citizenry of the United States today. We must take a careful look at what happened to Israel to understand what can; and, undoubtedly will, happen if we get what we want...change. Israel wanted a king to rule them like other nations. Men are again looking for a man to deliver them out of the perilous times in which we live. They are not looking to God. They do not want God's way, and like Israel, are finding the upheaval that comes when not choosing His way.

God told Samuel to *"...protest solemnly unto them, and show them the manner of the king that shall reign over them."* (1 Samuel 8:9) This nation, for one, has been warned time and again of its disobedience and rebellion. God-fearing prophets, preachers and teachers have cried long and, at times, loud, for repentance; but, it has fallen on deaf ears, and judgment will ensue.

What happened to Israel? Samuel told them exactly what would happen and it did down to the letter.

> *...This will be the manner of the king that shall reign over you: He will take your sons, and appoint them for himself, for his chariots, and to be his horsemen; and some shall run before his chariots.*
>
> *And he will appoint him captains over thousands, and captains over fifties; and will set them to ear his ground, and to reap his harvest, and to make his instruments of war, and instruments of his chariots.*
>
> *And he will take your daughters to be confectionaries, and to be cooks, and to be bakers.*

And he will take your fields, and your
vineyards, and your oliveyards, even the best
of them, and give them to his servants.

And he will take the tenth of your seed,
and of your vineyards, and give to his officers,
and to his servants.

And he will take your menservants,
and your maidservants, and your goodliest
young men, and your asses, and put them to
his work.

He will take the tenth of your sheep:
and ye shall be his servants.   And ye shall
cry out in that day because of your king which
ye shall have chosen you; and the Lord will
not hear you in that day.
(1 Samuel 8:11-18)

God's principles and laws are foundational for a
nation to experience peace and safety. He did not give them
to place people in harm's way; but, when they through their
own choosing, seek other avenues of help and strength,
He removes His hand and lets them have their own way.
Israel has more than once entered into the judgment of
the Lord, as has this nation. People cannot disobey the
Lord and expect to prosper. They may for a while, but
there will come a day of reckoning, and that day is fast
approaching. Even now it has passed over the threshold
and has entered our country, through the backdoor of crime,
drug trafficking, prostitution, pedophilia, illegal aliens and
corrupt government officials.

Nearly every nation on the face of the earth, is crying

out for a deliverer…still not seeking the King of kings and Lord of lords. Oh, yes, there is a remnant. God will not leave the people without a witness, no matter how they try to silence them, He will always raise up another, and another, and another; so, in the end, they can not say they have not been warned.

"Evil men and seducers shall wax worse and worse…" (2 Timothy 3:13) Day after day we have seen this scene escalating. While good men fear to speak up for fear of death; others cower in fear of the future, not realizing that even the judgments are in the hands of a loving God and that He is preparing the way for a new earth and new heaven free from sin and chaos. To do this, He must deal with the wicked, bringing judgment on them. Those judgments as dealt to the wicked, will have a profound effect on the righteous, as well. *"How shall we escape if we neglect so great salvation…".* (Hebrews 2:2)

Under King Saul's rule, the situation became so desperate the Israelites had to go to the Philistines to have their agricultural weapons of war sharpened…their rakes and shovels their fighting tools. They were reduced to nothing; and, all because they chose a king, who turned apostate, to rule over them. God gave them the desire of their heart, but disaster followed.

Throughout history, as we have seen, evil men ruling governments behind the scenes, have been deviates, manipulating and controlling people to suit their own purposes, led by the believer's adversary, Satan.

Sadly, we look on as we see our own nation in its death throes, not necessarily because we have hurt Israel; of course, that is a great part of it; but, rather, because Israel, according to prophecy will stand alone with only God as their defense in these final days. Their judgments will follow without any other nation to help, bringing Israel to its knees, and enabling them to recognize their Messiah, Jesus.

All nations will come under judgment for their treatment of God's people; and, not only nations, but individuals as well. Judgment will ensue not so much for ill treatment of the nation and people of Israel, but because they have broken the first commandment. *"Thou shalt have no other gods before Me."* (Exodus 20:3)

The United States has long forgotten her God. She has allowed the "shadow government" (a small group of wealthy elitists), to gain control over the nation in their ungodly efforts to rule the world, without so much as a whimper.

It matters not who is in power in these coming days for God's ultimate prophecies are unfolding at an alarming speed. Whoever is in power will, unknown to them, be following God's divine direction to bring the nations together for the Battle of Armageddon, which will destroy the ungodly and bring Jesus Christ back to earth to rule and reign.

When one realizes world leaders are only puppets in the hands of Lucifer, but God the director of the entire script in control, they will recognize the handwriting on the wall…that the time approaches when the adversaries of God will come to recognize His great and mighty power. Even though world leaders think they are in control, and their "god", greater than Almighty God, they will fall victim to His judgments.

> …*when thy judgments are in the earth, the inhabitants of the world will learn righteousness.*
>
> (Isaiah 26:9)

If one is not well-versed in God's word, they will not understand that these end-time events are not an individual matter, but the culmination of evil unleashed; the lawlessness one, Antichrist, being permitted his time. That snake in the Garden has slithered down through the centuries, and now is about to have his head smashed by one foot of the Lord Jesus Christ. Not before all have had a chance to make a choice, either for or against God.

God gave His very best; yet, even with that, men and women have chosen to go the way of the deceiver, liar, and murderer. For centuries, they have rejected the only One who could give them eternal peace and safety. They chose the short span spent on this earth, unwilling to pay the price for eternal life. While men of corrupt minds promised them freedom, liberty and peace, they, believed these liars, and by an act of their own will, chose another over their Creator.

Out of the jealousy, disobedience and rebellion of the

Sanhedrin and the overpowering, controlling government of Rome the sentence of death upon God's own Son was pronounced. These same, cruel, mocking spirits are alive today; their plans have not changed, they still want to do away with God-fearing people, and those who would interfere with the revival of the Old Roman Empire and the Ancient Mysteries of the cabala.

Those murderous individuals have lineage to the present-day Pharisees and Roman soldiers, presently revived and amassing under the banners of the European Union and United Nations. History does indeed repeat itself. Their evil spirits have been passed down from generation to generation (much like the Rothschild family), and their evil designs on the God-fearing are just as deadly, as in early Rome.

A showdown is coming. It had its onset at the rebirth of Israel, which coincides with the conception of the man whom many believe fills the shoes of an international fiend, the Antichrist.

Even if we could believe the depth of the wickedness of the men who have gone on before within the secret societies, we still may not be able to comprehend the extreme lawlessness and evil yet to come under Antichrist's reign. When killed, he will appear to come back to life, his body totally possessed by the devil. No one could begin to give a picture of his fiendish acts, so horribly gruesome they defy description. Yet, this world is about to fall into the hands of the worst despot of all. The restrainer is about to be unloosed.

Prince Charles has two coats of arms...one official and the other non-official. It is of note that in the non-official one, the restrainer's chain has been loosed, the hoof of the unicorn freed and kicking, and the dragon's foot touching the inner part of a circle, which represents the Sun god... all are symbols that Satan has gained control. The chain on his heraldry is known as the restrainer. (In the King James Version, the words. let or letteth are used in place of restrain or restrainer.) This is of interest in that when the restrainer of 2 Thessalonians 2:7 is loosed, so will all lawlessness. Assuredly, there will be looting, rioting, bombings, kidnappings and every evil manifestation the devil has devised.

Yet, in spite of all this evil and the horrendous, chaotic days yet to come, there is hope for the true Christian. Jesus is our hope, and our hope lies not on this earth, but beyond the grave wherein is peace, joy and love for all eternity.

Let's look at a possible scenario yet to be played out on the world scene. Please remember, the writer is not prophesying. This picture is not set in cement. It is only an idea of events to come.

The world is poised to receive anyone who claims and appears to deliver them out of chaos. As someone has said, they are looking for a deliverer, be they man or devil.

The United States is destined to become a lesser nation. Some believe this has been planned by the

Illuminati and their strategy teams for several years. Weakened by inner strife, financial upheaval, corrupt government, we will fall prey to becoming the third world country they so desire.   Freemasons sworn to fulfill their purposes on threat of horrible deaths if they fail to follow orders are already in place, as are infiltrators within clubs, organizations and churches prepared to carry out their plans.

Some…Shriners…have sworn allegiance to Allah, whether deceived and unknowing, or willfully. Others are ignorant, but all are ignorant of Satan's devices, or they would never have sworn allegiance by taking secret oaths demanding total obedience and adherence to their Order's laws, whatever Order they are under.

Secret societies are rife in every nation. Now, with national leaders at their helm, they have steadily moved into place on the world stage. A Muslim, or Illuminist, in office will bring this nation into slavery such as we have never known, crippling us and opening the doors for U. N. takeover. We will then be powerless to help Israel.

Although a false peace may first ensue, putting the people off guard, saying, "peace and safety", sudden destruction looms on the horizon. Russia is again rattling their sabers, arming their allies, and keeping the United States blinded to future movements. Their allies, the nations of Kazakhstan, Kyrgyzstan, Uzbekistan, Turkmenistan, Tajikistan, and parts of Afghanistan, Turkey, Germany, Austria, Iran, Ethiopia, Turkey, Iraq and Lybia follow the Islamic religion. Under Russian pressure, these combined forces are scheduled to march down upon the mountains of Israel, where they will be destroyed. Called the battle of Gog and Magog in Ezekiel 38 and 39, it is actually World War III.

As the war lords mingle in preparation for this battle, Israel recognizes that it is the target of the Gog and Magog war about to ensue, and are attempting to prepare as much as this little nation can. They may be small, but with God's help the Russian invasion will be stopped on the mountains of Israel. God will be sanctified before the heathen...the Islamic nations; and, only a sixth of the Russian army will survive. (Ezekiel 38:16 and 39:2) If you're afraid of the Islams, remember it's all in God's hands. They may appear to be winning, but they are not!

Not only will the Israelis be busy for the next seven years...covering the period of the Great Tribulation or Jacob's Trouble, during which time they are burying their dead, the heathen will have an awakening, realizing that there is a God not made by hands. This may be the time of the great revival so many have proclaimed, as God will be sanctified in the heathen's eyes. The nation of Israel, however, will endure a severe shaking.

The Dome of the Rock, which must be leveled for the rebuilding of the temple, may be leveled through this great shaking; and, the Arabs which have held the mount, would no longer in a position to claim it. This makes the way not only for the rebuilding of the temple, but for the Antichrist to rise to power saying he has all the answers. Inasmuch as the last week of Daniel's 70th week must take place (the time of Jacob's Trouble), and sacrifices offered again in the temple, the Levitical priesthood and institution of ceremonial law will revive.

The Illuminati/Freemason Antichrist will set his feet first upon the ruins on the temple mount and eventually proclaim himself "God", offering a polluted sacrifice on the temple altar, as did Antiochus Epiphanes. When this happens, the Israelites will recognize they have been deceived, and those in Judea will "run for the hills", knowing destruction is about to follow. (Revelation 24:16) Jews throughout Israel during this entire tribulation period are turning to Jesus, proclaiming Him Lord and Savior.

What follows will be a time of merciless bloodletting. Those who refuse to take the Mark of the Beast, and worship the Antichrist will be martyred. Many believers will lay down their lives for the cause of Christ Jesus, once and for all overcoming the "accuser of the brethren".

A mighty destruction falls upon both religious and political Babylon. Angered by its destruction, Israel is blamed; and, armies from the world over encircle Israel prepared for the Battle of Armageddon, determined to annihilate Israel and their God. These armies are led and inspired by demonic hordes.

As the plan of the ages erupts in a dynamic finish, the last trumpet sounds, (Revelation 11:15) and Jesus Christ, the Lord of Lords and King of Kings sets his feet upon land and sea, as the kingdoms of this world become the kingdoms of our Lord and His Christ. With the entrance of Jesus, the sword of His mouth defeats the Antichrist and his vast armies, and the blood flows to the horses' bridles.

Then tremendous upheavals erupt in the earth as the Lord makes way to prepare for the new heavens and the new earth…it is the time of God's wrath, and the final destruction of all the wicked and unrepentant of earth. As a child of God, you may come under Satan's wrath, but never God's. Chastisement maybe yes, but wrath no!

Are you ready? Have you made your peace with God, or have you been blinded by sin and rebellion? Now is the time of salvation…now is the accepted time. Don't delay. Repent and receive the Lord as your Savior before you fall into the hands of an angry God.

> *And they shall be mine, saith the Lord of hosts, in that day when I make up my jewels; and I will spare them, as a man spareth his own son that serveth him. Then shall ye return, and discern between the righteous and the wicked, between him that serveth God and him that serveth him not.*
>
> (Malachi 3:17-18)
>
> *For, behold, the day cometh, that shall burn as an oven; and all the proud, yea, and all that do wickedly, shall be stubble: and the day that cometh shall burn them up, saith the Lord of hosts, that it shall leave them neither root nor branch. But unto you that fear my name shall the Sun of righteousness arise with healing in*

his wings; and ye shall go forth, and grow up as calves of the stall. And ye shall tread down the wicked; for they shall be ashes under the soles of your feet in the day that I shall do this, saith the Lord of hosts.

(Malachi 4:1-3)

He will arise in great glory upon the remnant bride, who willingly have taken their cross to follow Him. Believers will be vindicated among the nations and raised up as kings and priests unto Him.

God is Sovereign. He has the final say, and is the One who judges both the quick and the dead. Don't be caught dead without Him! If you have not accepted Jesus as your Savior and repented of your sins, then please pray the following prayer:

Father, I have sinned in that I have neglected to accept your Son. and receive forgiveness of my many sins. I deeply regret that I have been willful and disobedient to your Word. Forgive my heart of unbelief and accept me into your Kingdom. I repent and turn my back on my sins. In Jesus' Name, Amen.

GLOSSARY

Adept…One who shows knowledge, skill or aptitude in magic.

Alchemy. Alchemical…A medieval chemical science, in which it was believed to be able to change base metals into gold and to discover a cure for diseases and means of indefinitely prolonging life. Pharmacology developed from this belief; hence, the use of mind-altering drugs for the purpose of control. Illuminists believe by psychology and mind control they are able to change the character of humanity.

Ancient Mysteries…Mystical rites that evolved from the knowledge of good and evil; also known as Gnosticism.

Apostasy…A total departure from one's faith or religion; can also apply to politics.

Ashkenazi… Jewish "pretenders"; see Khazars

Ashteroth…Mythological goddesses of Babylon, aka Isis, Astarte and Ishtar.

Beltane…A Celtic, occult holiday, observed with fertility rituals, accompanied by bonfires.

Baphomet…a name given the Goat of Mendes, or as in the OTO's Gnostic Mass, the serpent, lion, or mystery of mysteries; i.e., Satan.

Bestiality…Sex acts with animals.

Bilderbergers...A secret society created in 1954 with the goal of World Government. This group is the crème de la creme.

Cabala....Occult Jewish philosophy found in the Talmud. Also see Kabbalah.

Council on Foreign Relations...3,000 member group who strongly promotes a One World Government and augment the plans of the financial elitists behind it.

Cryptocracy (ies)...Secret society (ies).

Cult...A religious sect considered extreme or false, led by a charismatic, authoritarian figure.

Eschatology...Theology concerning end-time prophecies.

Freemasonry (Masons; Masonry)...A secret fraternal organization based on Egyptology. (Egyptian worship of gods and goddesses) and considered a "religion" by their core members. It is complete with a Bible containing their own commentary.

Globalism...Another name for the One World Government.

Gnosticism...Taken from the Greek word, gnosis, which means knowledge. Gnostics accept religions devoid of belief in One God, whom they believe to be imperfect. This knowledge (of good and evil) found its way into Babylon and Egypt, then the Jewish Talmud. Early believers were given warning about its antichrist teaching by John the Beloved, in 1 John 4. Many heretical Bible versions have been derived.

Hegelian Principle…A principle that first creates a problem, then publicizes it, and then offers its own solution to the advantage of those who employ it.

Heresy…A corruption of true, Christian faith.

Hexagram…A six-sided, double triangle, used in witchcraft rites.

Horus…A "god" considered the son of Osiris, who gave his "eye" to Osiris, and from where the name "all-seeing eye" originated.

Illuminati…An overseeing body of major secret societies, meaning the "illumined ones," those with special knowledge (in the mysteries).

Ishtar…A mother goddess worshipped by practitioners of Islam, one of many names for Astarte, Isis or Ashtoreth,

Islam…An religion founded on the principles of Muhammad. Islam rightfully claims lineage from Abraham through Ishmael. They worship Allah and claim that he is the One God. Allah is not the God of the Bible…Yahweh.

Judaism; Judaizers…Apostate Jews---those who promote the apostate Jewish ideals. Also, those who, according to Scripture delivered Jesus to Herod for crucifixion.. They follow the Talmud and Cabala. They believe they are a superior race and deserve special privileges. See Zion, Zionists and Zionism.

Kabbalah… A group of sacred books of black magic of Orthodox Judaism that form in large part the basis of secret societies,

Khazars…Pseudo-Jews aka Ashkenazi Jews…a Turk-Mongol people who converted to Judaism.

Lucifer aka Satan…A created being—a cherubim— who apostatized and willed to usurp the throne of God. He is considered Jesus' brother by Mormons (Latter Day Saints) and Masons of higher rites.

Metaphysics…An idea or a doctrine not recognized (understood) in the physical sense realm or by logic..

Nimrod…A mighty hunter as shown in Genesis, whom history has disclosed ruled over the now known Arab world.   He and his mother were instrumental in the development of the Babylonian religion and Egyptology, which has become known as "Babylon, the Great" in Revelation 17.

Nod…Land east of Eden where Cain moved. It means, "wandering."

Order of the Garter…A British order for knighthood. It also covertly encompasses witchcraft covens and is a cover organization for secret societies.

Ordo Templi Orientis (OTO)…A covert organization that claims to be the hierarchy of Freemasonry. Its rites are extremely evil, promoting extreme sexual perversion, animal and human sacrifice.

Osiris…Mythological father of Horus. See Horus.

Pentagram…Five-pointed star of witchcraft rites. Also used to denote Baphomet, the Goat of Mendes, or Satan.

Prophecy…A foretelling of future events.

Psychology...The mental science of the soul, or "psyche," as opposed to the spirit, "pneuma."

Reincarnation....An Eastern/New Age doctrine that believes when an individual dies they will return to earth in another form; thereby, giving them the opportunity to redeem themselves from any former deviant behavior.

Sanhedrin...The judicial body of Israel's Supreme Court and adherents of the Talmud.

Semiramis...Nimrod's mother, who became known as Babylon, "Mother of Harlots." Worshipped today under the presumptuous name of Mary, mother of God; or as in the Merovingian Dynasty, Mary, mother of gods.

Skull and Bones...A secret society that takes its orders and leading from the Illuminati. Their rites include a pseudo-burial in a casket and then, upon rising from the casket, are said to be "born again." This follows the ancient rites of Osiris. The worship of skulls and bones is found among occult groups.

Trilateral Commission...An affiliated arm of the Illuminati, a small think tank that works together to enable the establishment of the New World Order.

Unity...Unity denies faith in Jesus Christ and His finished work as the way ofalvation. It is pantheistic, believes that God and the Universe are one and God is, therefore, not the Creator. It is metaphysical practices abstract meditation.

Witchcraft...The result of rebellion, naturally

follows apostasy. Simply put, these invoke demonic powers to carry out their desires through superstitious rites.

<u>Ziggurat</u>…Pyramid-type structures in which Gnostic rituals were performed during the time of Nimrod.

<u>Zion, Zionist, Zionism</u>…A person belonging to an organization originally formed to gather together Jews into one homeland. This movement was ultimately taken over and controlled by wealthy Judaic Jews. A Zionist may be unaware of the evil designs of Satanic Zionists. As is often the case, in order to deceive the masses, a word with one meaning may mean the exact opposite to serve the Order's purpose. Such is the case with Zion which within the Word of God normally refers to the church and or the Hebrew people.

Preface

1. Note the occult date. The same day as the towers were destroyed in 2001.
2. Ethelbert W. Bullinger, DD., *Number in Scripture,* (New York, NY, Cosimo, Inc., 2005), p. 235.
3. Ibid. p. 253.
4. Ibid. p. 257.
5. See Chapter 12.
6. William Whiston, A..D., Translator of *The Complete Works of Josephus,* (Grand Rapids, MI., Kregel Publications, 1991), p. 27.
7. Ibid.
8. Ibid.
9. See Glossary.
10. The spelling of *"cabala"* will be used throughout this book, rather than the multiplicity of spellings.
11. *Early Modern History, (1450-1789),* American Heritage Dictionary, 2007, http://www.dictionary.reference.com/help/ahd4.htm.
12. John Daniel, *Scarlet and the Beast,* (Longview, TX., Day Publishing, 2007), p. 582.
13. Note: An easy way to understand the Trinity is the example of an egg. An egg has a shell (a body), egg white (light and that which

evaporates easily), and a yolk, which is the heart of all. Together they are one, but each having a different function.

14. Whiston, translator of *The Complete Works of Josephus,* p. 27.
15. Alexander Hislop, *The Two Babylons,* (New York, NY., Loizeaux Brothers, 1959), p. 276.
16. Ibid. p. 304.
17. Ibid. p. 316.
18. Whiston, translator of *The Complete Works of Josephus,* p. 30.
19. Ibid.
20. Wanda Marrs, *New Age Lies to Women,* (Austin, TX., Living Truth Publishers, 1989), p. 38.
21. Hislop, *The Two Babylons,* pp. 76-77.
22. Marrs, *New Age Lives to Women,* p. 115.
23. Jone Johnson Lewis, *Worship of Semiramis,* August 2006, *http://*www.womenshistory.about.com.
24. Marrs, *New Age Lies to Women,* p. 130.
25. Fritz Springmeier, *Bloodlines of the Illuminati*, (Austin, TX., Ambassador House, 1998), p. 291.
26. See Glossary.
27. Springmeier, *Bloodlines of the Illuminati,* p. 291.
28. Ibid. p. 370.
29. Joseph Carr, *The Twisted Cross*, (Shreveport, Huntington House, LA.,1985), p. 197
30. Springmeier, *Bloodlines of the Illuminati,* p.136.

31. *Received Text vs. Deceived Text*, 2007, *http://www.888webtoday.com/leroy100.html.*

32. Texe Marrs, *Codex Magica*, (Austin, TX., RiverCrest Publishing, 2005), p. 433.

33. Andrew Carrington Hitchcock, *The Synagogue of Satan*, (Austin, TX., RiverCrest, 2007), p. 8.

34. *Received Text vs. Deceived Text,* (2007), *http://www.888webtoday.com/leroy100.html*

35. Ibid.

36. Ibid.

37. Ibid.

38. Ibid.

39. Rev. Charles Salliby, *If the Foundations Be Destroyed*, (Fiskdale, MA., Word and Prayer Ministries, 1994), p. 65.

40. Frederick Clarkson, 2007 *Christian Reconstruction's Theocratic Dominion Gains Influence, http://www.tylwytheg.com/enemies/recontruct2.html.*

41. Dr. Larry Spargimino, Ph.D., *"Smuggling Gnostic Theology into the Church Through Modern Versions,"* (Oklahoma City; OK., "The Prophetic Observer Newsletter" Vol.15, No. 2, 2008). p. 1.

42. Ibid.

43. Clarkson, 2007 *Christian Reconstruction's Theocratic Dominion Gains Influence, http://www.tylwytheg.com/enemies/recontruct2.html*

44. Ibid.

45. Springmeier, *Bloodlines of the Illuminati,* p.

291.

46. Ibid. p. 292.
47. Tim Cohen, *The Antichrist and a Cup of Tea,* (Aurora, CO., Prophecy, House, 1998), p. 301.
48. Craig, Heimbichner, *Blood on the Altar,* (Coeur d' Alene, ID., 2005), p. 9.
49. Rutherford H. Platt, Jr., Editor, 2007, The Forgotten Book of Eden:The Testament of Dan, Chapter 2 , Sacred Texts Bible Apocrapha, *http://www.sacred-texts.com/ bib/fbe/index.htm.*
50. Marrs, Texe, Codex Magica, p. 247.
51. J. R Church, *Guardians of the Grail,* (Oklahoma City, OK., Prophecy Publications, 1991), p. 119.
52. Springmeier, *Bloodlines of the Illuminati*, p. 373.
53. Janet Moser, 2007, *The Lost Tribe of Dan: The Early Jewish and Christian View of the Identification of the Anti-Christ* http://www. watch.pair.com/dan.html.
54. Church, *Guardians of the Grail*, p. 113.
55. Ibid. p. 114.
56. Clarence Larkin, *The Book of Revelation,* (Glenside, PA., Clarence Larkin Estate, 1919), p. 20.
57. Ibid. p. 46.
58. Ibid.
59. Jessie Penn-Lewis, *War on the Saints*, (New York, NY, Thomas E. Lowe, Ninth Edition, 1973), p. 22.

60. Ibid.
61. Marrs, Texe, *Codex Magica*, p. 39.
62. Kirban, Salem, *Satan's Angels Exposed,* (Huntington Valley, PA., Salem Kirban, Inc., 1980), p. 161.
63. Daniel, *Scarlet and the Beast,* p. 31.
64. Finney, Charles, *The Character, Claims and Practical Workings of Freemasonry,* Introduction by John Daniel, (Longview, TX., Day Publishing, 1998), p. lxiii.
65. Ibid. pp. xxiii-xxiv.
66. Marrs, Texe, *Codex Magica,* p. 43.
67. Ibid. pp. 43-44.
68. David Bay, citing *Egypt Cradle of Ancient Masonry by* Fredrick de Clifford, http://www.cuttingedge.com.
69. Ibid.
70. Finney, *The Character, Claims and Practical Workings of Freemasonry,* Introduction by John Daniel, quoting from the Masonic Hand Book, p. xxxiv.
71. Kirban, *Satan's Angels Exposed,* p, 147.
72. Hitchcock, *The Synagogue of Satan,* p. 32
73. See Glossary.
74. Hitchcock, *The Synagogue of Satan,* p. 33.
75. Ibid. 33-35.
76. Finney, *The Character, Claims and Practical Workings of Freemasonry,* Introduction by John Daniel, p. lxx.
77. Kirban, *Satan's Angels Exposed,* p. 147.
78. Ibid. p. 149.
79. Ibid.

80. Ibid.
81. Ibid. p.150.
82. Ibid.
83. Ibid. p. 148.
84. Ibid.
85. Ibid.
86. Ibid.
87. Springmeier, *Bloodlines of the Illuminati,* p. 13.
88. Kirban, *Satan's Angels Exposed,* p. 151.
89. Ibid.
90. Springmeier, *Bloodlines of the Illuminati,* p. 368.
91. Ibid.
92. Kirban, Satan's Angels Exposed, p. 157.
93. Note:...Marx was a crypto-Jew. His real name was Moses Levy Mordecai, or in some instances it was given as Mordecai Levi.
94. Finney, The Character, Claims and Practical Workings of Freemasonry,   Introduction by John Daniel , p. lxvii.
95. Kirban, Satan's Angels Exposed, p. 151.
96. Springmeier, Bloodlines of the Illuminati, p.13.
97. Kirban, Satan's Angels Exposed, p. 149.
98. Smith, The History of God's People and the Coming New World Order, p. 153.
99. Kirban, *Satan's Angels Exposed,* p. 151.
100. Ibid. p. 159.
101. Ibid. pp. 162-163.
102. Springmeier, *Bloodlines of the Illuminati,* p. 194.

103. Ibid. p. 2.

104. Ibid. p. 372.

105. Ibid. p. 369.

106. Note: Bees were associated with Samson, who found a hive of bees within the lion he had slain. (Judges 14:8) Samson was of the tribe of Dan, and this is only one of the clues as to Dan's involvement within the Merovingian monarchies.

107. Springmeier, *Bloodlines of the Illuminati,* p. 373.

108. Ibid. Table of Contents.

109. Springmeier, *Bloodlines of the Illuminati,* p. 108.

110. Ibid. p. 381.

111. Ibid. p. 273.

112. The "Fed" here refers to the Federal Reserve.

113. Hitchcock, *The Synagogue of Satan,* p. 37.

114. Ibid.

115. Hitchcock, *The Synagogue of Satan, q*uoting Otto Von Bismarck, p. 63..

116. Ibid. p. 65.

117. Ibid.

118. Ibid. p. 69.

119. See Glossary.

120. Hitchcock, *The Synagogue of Satan,* p. 145.

121. O. J. Graham, *The Six-Pointed Star* (Fairview, NC, New Puritan Library, 1984), citing *Encyclopaedia Judaica,* p. 29.

122. Bay, *Freemasonry Proven to Worship Lucifer,* Part 2*, www. cuttingedge. com.,*quoting Mary Ann Slipper, *The*

Symbolism of Order of the Eastern Star,
p.14.

123. Ibid.

124. Graham, *The Six-Pointed Star,* quoting
Richard Siegel and Carl Rheims,
*Metamorphoses of a Tree: 10 Jewish
Symbols and Their Meanings,* p. 19.

125. Ibid. p.12.

126. Ibid. p. 22.

127. See Chapter 12, *"The Ordo Templi Orientis,
or OTO."*

128. Heimbichner, *Blood on the Altar,* p. 13.

129. Italics added for emphasis.

130. Graham, *The Six-Pointed Star,* 36; quoting
Jack Chick, *Spellbound,* Chick Publications,
pp. 13-14.

131. Hitchcock, *The Synagogue of Satan*, p.155.

132. Graham, *The Six-Pointed Star,* p. 91.

133. Bay, *Freemasonry Proven to Worship
Lucifer,* Part 2, *http://www. cuttingedge.com.*

134. Marrs, Texe, *Codex Magica,* p. 540.

135. Springmeier, *Bloodlines of the Illuminati,* p.
228.

136. Ibid. pp. 236-237.

137. Ibid. p. 371.

138. Hitchcock, *The Synagogue of Satan,p.* p. 12.

139. Springmeier, *Bloodlines of the Illuminati,* p.
242.

140. Ibid. p. 371.

141. Ibid. p. 237.

142. Ibid.

143. See Glossary.

144. Springmeier, *Bloodlines of the Illuminati,* p. 237.

145. Graham, *The Six-Pointed Star,* p. 51.

146. Ibid. p. 52.

147. Ibid. p. 66.

148. Springmeier, *Bloodlines of the Illuminati,* p. 260.

149. Ibid. p. 239.

150. Hitchcock, *The Synagogue of Satan,* p. 49.

151. Note: For more information and picture proofs of this, the reader is invited to view the following article, written by Jerry Golden, within the following website: *The Root of Evil in Jerusalem, http://*www. thegoldenreport.com.

152. Church, *Guardians of the Grail,* p. 115.

153. Note: The words *letteth* and *let* can be defined as "restrains" and "restrain." In other words, lawlessness will prosper when the restrainer is removed.

154. Carr, *The Twisted Cross,* p. 197.

155. Heimbichner, *Blood on the Altar,* p. 96.

156. Note: There is no certainty that Benjamin Franklin actually adhered to the total debauchery of that club. He was known to be a ladies' man; however, it has also been surmised that he may have been an agent for the new colonies…and even a double spy… working for King George III, while giving information to the colonists. Espionage was indeed possible in the early days of the United States, as it is today.

157. Heimbichner, *Blood on the Altar,* p. 11.
158. Ibid. p. 14.
159. Ibid. p. 30.
160. Ray Thomas, *The Hegelian Principle*, *http://* www.geocities.com/thomasreport/hegelian. html.
161. See Glossary.
162. Heimbichner, *Blood on the Altar,* p. 13.
163. Ibid. p. 35.
164. Ibid. p. 14.
165. See Glossary.
166. Lisa Renee, *Father Gerald Robinson Murder Trial*, *http://robinsonmurdertrial.blogspot. com.*
167. Alex Jones, *The Bohemian Grove and the Global Elite, Archive Coverage,* (2007). *http://*www.prisonplanet.com.
168. Italics added for emphasis.
169. Heimbichner, *Blood on the Altar,* p. 14.
170. Ibid. pp. 21-22.
171. Ibid. p. 25.
172. Ibid. p. 29.
173. See Glossary.
174. Ibid. pp. 29-30.
175. Ibid. p. 114.
176. Ibid. p. 115.
177. Ibid. p. 114.
178. Ibid. p. 117.
179. Kirban, *Satan's Angels Exposed*, p.149.
180. Available through Prophecy House, Inc., P. O. Box. 461104, Aurora, CO 80046.
181. Church, *Guardians of the Grail,* p. 98.

182. Hislop, *The Two Babylons,* p. 269.
183. Smith, *The History of God's People and the Coming New World Order*, p. 71.
184. Tim Cohen, *The Antichrist and a Cup of Tea,* p. 58.
185. Ibid. p. 35.
186. Ibid. p. 201.
187. Ibid. p. 255.
188. Ibid. p. 301.
189. Ibid.
190. Springmeier, *Bloodlines of the Illuminati*, p. 373.
191. Bay, *Cutting Edge Newsletter,* Special News Alert, January 4, 2008; *http://www. cuttingedge.org.*